ALSO BY CHRIS HEDGES

War Is a Force That Gives Us Meaning

WHAT EVERY PERSON SHOULD KNOW ABOUT WAR

CHRIS HEDGES

FREE PRESS

NEW YORK LONDON TORONTO SYDNEY

FREE PRESS
A Division of Simon & Schuster, Inc.
1230 Avenue of the Americas
New York, NY 10020

First Free Press trade paperback edition 2003

FREE PRESS and colophon are registered trademarks of
Simon & Schuster, Inc.

For information regarding special discounts for bulk purchases,
please contact Simon & Schuster Special Sales at 1-800-456-6798
or business@simonandschuster.com

Designed by Joseph Rutt

Manufactured in the United States of America

10 9 8 7 6

Library of Congress Cataloging-in-Publication Data is available.

ISBN 0-7432-5512-7

For my children, Thomas and Noëlle, and yours

There is ful many a man that crieth "Werre! Werre!"
that woot ful litel what werre amounteth.

> —Geoffrey Chaucer, medieval English poet
> who was a soldier and prisoner of war in
> France, in "The Tale of Melibee,"
> *The Canterbury Tales*, c. 1392

CONTENTS

INTRODUCTION

I have spent most of my adult life reporting war. By the time it was over, after nearly two decades, I had worked as a correspondent in about a dozen conflicts from Central America to Africa to the Middle East and the Balkans. I spent five years covering the insurgencies in El Salvador, Guatemala, and Nicaragua. I was there for the first Palestinian uprising, or intifada, in the West Bank and Gaza, and returned to write about the second. I reported on the civil wars in the Sudan and Yemen, the uprisings in Algeria and the Punjab, and the collapse of the communist regimes in East Germany, Czechoslovakia, and Romania. I went on to the Gulf War, the Kurdish rebellion in southeastern Turkey and northern Iraq, the war in Bosnia, and finally to the fighting in Kosovo.

I have been in ambushes on desolate dirt roads in Central America, in firefights in the marshes in southern Iraq between Shiite rebels and Iraqi soldiers, imprisoned in the Sudan, captured and held prisoner for a week by the Iraqi Republican Guard in Basra during the Shiite rebellion following the 1991 Gulf War, strafed by MiG-21s in Bosnia, fired upon by Serb snipers, and pounded with over 1,000 heavy shells a day in Sarajevo. I struggle with the demons all who have been to war must bear. There are days when these burdens seem more than I can handle.

There are few books that describe in raw detail the effects of war, what it does to bodies, to minds and souls. The trauma of war is often too hard for us to digest. We find it easier to believe the myths about war, the exciting call to duty, honor, courage, and glory, those abstract terms that are rendered hollow in combat. This is not to say these qualities do not exist—they do—but they rarely have much place on the battlefield. Modern industrial warfare is largely impersonal. The effects of these powerful weapons and explosives on human bodies are usually not disclosed to the public. The physical and psychological wounds are lifelong crucibles carried by veterans and civilian survivors. These wounds are often unseen. Those who suffer from war's touch are often left to struggle with the awful scars of war alone or with their families. War, when we understand it, forces us to confront our own capacity for violence, indeed for atrocity. And it is little wonder that most of us prefer to turn away.

"Few of us can hold on to our real selves long enough to discover the momentous truths about ourselves and this whirling earth to which we cling," wrote J. Glenn Gray, a combat veteran of World War II, in *The Warriors: Reflections on Men in Battle.* "This is especially true of men in war. The great god Mars tries to blind us when we enter his realm, and when we leave he gives us a generous cup of the waters of Lethe to drink."

We ennoble war. We turn it into entertainment. And in all this we forget what war is about, what it does to those who wage it and those who suffer from it. We ask those in the military and their families to make sacrifices that color the rest of their lives. Those who hate war the most, I have often found, are veterans who know it.

War, I believe, is an inevitable part of the human condition. I doubt it will ever be eradicated. But it should never be waged lightly or without good cause. The cost is high. Most of those killed, wounded, and left homeless in modern warfare are innocents, families, including children. There are millions of people on this planet who, because of war, have been thrust into a life of want and misery. And their dislocation, along with their loss of dignity and basic human rights, has created legions of the disenfranchised.

The truth about war is hard to confront, especially if we have come to believe the romantic image of war. But the truth will arm us to wage war. It will make us conscious of the sacrifices we demand from those we send to fight. Our young men and women do not deserve to be deceived about the difficulties they must undertake. In a democracy, the voting public must grasp the exacting toll of war. And when we know what it is we face, and the possible consequences, we will be better prepared to cope with the stress, pain, and loss. Those who come back from war will be better able to handle their own trauma. They will understand that they are not alone. Perhaps they will also come to realize that we all need help. We all need each other. War is a cross no one should have to bear alone.

"Give sorrow words," William Shakespeare wrote, "The grief that does not speak whispers the o'erfraught heart and bids it break."

The book is a manual on war. There is no rhetoric. There are very few adjectives. It is a book based on research. The core of the research was directed by Cabe Franklin, who worked with Sam Frank and Byrd Schas. Laurie Kelliher, along with some of my other graduate students at Columbia University's School of Journalism, gave many hours to the effort. The book is also the product of a great deal of reflection by several veterans, especially John Wheeler who graduated from West Point, served in Vietnam, and went on to chair the drive to build the Vietnam Veterans Memorial in Washington, D.C. He significantly shaped and molded the book. Paul Woodruff, a philosopher who wrote *Reverence: Renewing a*

Forgotten Virtue and was a military adviser in Vietnam, helped edit the manuscript. The novelist Christian Bauman, who joined the Army after high school and served in Somalia and Haiti, along with Jarrad Shiver, who was a sergeant in the Marine Corps, made sure the concerns and dilemmas of the enlisted men and women were included. Christian wrote *The Ice Beneath You*, one of the finest books on life in the American army. And we are indebted to three members of the Hughes family, all West Point graduates, who helped us look at the issues that concern women in the military and made sure we thoughtfully asked and answered questions about wounds and warfare. Carolyn Hughes Copenhaver, a former Army captain who served in military intelligence from 1992 to 1997, Captain John R. Hughes, an Army surgeon, and Dr. William F. Hughes, a retired colonel who served three tours in Vietnam, all generously lent their expertise to the work.

We drew up basic questions about war and searched medical, psychological, and military studies for information. We were meticulous about footnotes, fact checking, and sourcing. If anyone wants more on any subject, the footnotes and bibliography show where to find it. We kept the book direct and accessible. And we operated on the assumption that the simplest and most obvious questions in life, and certainly war, often never get asked. The ancient Greek philosopher Heracleitus noted that "men are estranged from what is most familiar and they must seek out what is in itself evident."

The idea for the book came from the work of Harold Roland Shapiro, a New York lawyer who stumbled on medical studies from World War I during a law case. The medical descriptions, he wrote, rendered "all that I had read and heard previously as being either fiction, isolated reminiscence, vague generalization or deliberate propaganda."

He began to do research in the New York Academy of Medicine and the Association of the Bar of the City of New

York. He published a book called *What Every Young Man Should Know About War* (Knight Publishers, Inc., 1937) in question-and-answer format. The book was published a year later in London by George Allen and Unwin Ltd. It described war in "dispassionate words" that were "as irrevocable as bullets once they have been issued from the mouth of a machine gun."

Mr. Shapiro, who hoped to avert another war, distributed his book on the eve of World War II. But when the war started, fearing that it would interfere with recruiting, he pulled the few copies in circulation. The book never appeared in print again.

Lawrence Walsh, who covered the war in Afghanistan, mentioned the book to me while I was on a Nieman Fellowship at Harvard. It was hard to find. Widener Library at Harvard, the second largest in the country, did not have a copy. I had to order it from the Library of Congress.

The book is dated. It deals with bayonet wounds, "trench fever," and "going over the top." And it pulls almost exclusively from medical studies. Its focus is on physical wounds, although one sees glimpses of the recognition of the deep psychological cost of war in vague medical references to "anxiety state." However limited, the concept was brilliant. And Mr. Shapiro, who died in 1985, did his country a great service. I want to thank his son, Dr. Jonathan S. Shapiro, for sharing with me his father's history and blessing our enterprise.

A lot of work has been done on the physical and psychological effects of war since World War I. Post-traumatic stress disorder, for example, was not officially recognized and named until after the Vietnam War. We now have a much better understanding of what the trauma of war does to us. But the military has also worked hard to make its soldiers more efficient killers. It has employed the tools of science, technology, and psychology to increase the lethal force of combat units. These studies strip away the gloss of military life. There is a method to the military's madness. And recruits will be better able to cope with what seems like insanity when they understand what it is the military is trying to accomplish.

Finally, there may be some who dislike this book. It is hard to read. But war is hard. And closing our eyes to the reality of war will not make it go away, nor will it make it better. Knowledge does give us power. It allows us to understand what is being done to us. It allows us to prepare ourselves for the hard task of warfare. It makes us cautious and hopefully hesitant about unleashing the dogs of war. Most important, it gives us a greater compassion and insight toward those who return from war. The invisible wounds inflicted on survivors are potent. They can destroy lives, long after the conflict has ended, as effectively as artillery shells.

This book is meant to give a glimpse into war as it is, not as it is usually portrayed by the entertainment industry, the state, and the press. War, however inevitable and necessary, must always be a final resort. It is always tragic. War maims generations. War sends out deadly aftershocks that ripple outward in ways we do not understand. War, the blood-swollen god, asks us to sacrifice our young. Beware of that sacrifice. Fear it.

—Chris Hedges
New York City, April 2003

Chapter 1

WAR 101

What is a war?

War is defined as an active conflict that has claimed more than 1,000 lives.[1]

Has the world ever been at peace?

Of the past 3,400 years, humans have been entirely at peace for 268 of them, or just 8 percent of recorded history.[2]

How many people have died in war?

At least 108 million people were killed in wars in the twentieth century. Estimates for the total number killed in wars throughout all of human history range from 150 million to 1 billion. War has several other effects on population, including decreasing the birthrate by taking men away from their wives. The reduced birthrate during World War II is estimated to have caused a population deficit of more than 20 million people.[3]

How many people around the world serve in the military?

The combined armed forces of the world have 21.3 million people. China has the world's largest, with 2.4 million. America is second with 1.4 million. India has 1.3 million, North Korea

1 million, and Russia 900,000. Of the world's 20 largest militaries, 14 are in developing nations.[4]

How many wars are taking place right now?

At the beginning of 2003 there were 30 wars going on around the world. These included conflicts in Afghanistan, Algeria, Burundi, China, Colombia, the Congo, India, Indonesia, Israel, Iraq, Liberia, Nigeria, Pakistan, Peru, the Philippines, Russia, Somalia, Sudan, and Uganda.[5]

Is there a genetic reason why we fight?

There is no single "war gene." Combinations of genes can predispose a person to violence. However, aggression is a product of biology and environment. In America, sources of aggressive dispositions include domestic violence, the portrayal of violence in the media, threats from enemies, and combat training.[6]

Is war essentially male?

Worldwide, 97 percent of today's military personnel are male. This is thought to be a reflection of culture and biology. Fifteen percent (204,000) of American military personnel are female.[7]

Can women fight as effectively as men do?

Yes. While fewer women are "natural killers," and women are on average smaller than men, there are many women who have the psychological makeup and the physical ability to fight. There are many men without either. Women have shown valor in combat. Dr. Mary Walker won the Medal of Honor during the Civil War.[8]

Why are civilians so attracted to war?

War is often regarded by observers as honorable and noble.

It can be viewed as a contest between nations, a chance to compete and be declared the victor.[9]

Does the American public support war?

Between 65 and 85 percent of the American public will support a military action when it begins. Vietnam had 64 percent support in 1965. As American casualties mount, support often decreases. The Korean and Vietnam Wars ended with support levels near 30 percent. World War II support levels never fell below 77 percent, despite the prolonged and damaging nature of the conflict. The Gulf War enjoyed similar levels of support.[10]

How large is the American military?

The active peacetime force of the U.S. armed services includes 1.4 million people, with the Army making up almost 500,000 of that number. The Navy has approximately 380,000 men and women on active duty. The Air Force has approximately 365,000, and the Marines have approximately 175,000. Approximately 1.3 million Americans serve in Reserve and National Guard branches that can be activated in time of war.[11]

How many Americans have died in wars?

More than 650,000 Americans have been killed in combat. Another 243,000 have died while wars were being fought, due to training accidents, injury, and disease. In the twentieth century, approximately 53,000 Americans were killed in combat in World War I, 291,000 in World War II, 33,000 in the Korean War, 47,000 in Vietnam, and 148 in the Gulf War. Including deaths from disease, accidents, and other factors, each war's total was much higher: approximately 116,000 died in World War I, 400,000 in World War II, 53,000 in the Korean War, 90,000 in Vietnam, and almost 400 in the Gulf War.[12]

How deadly is the American military?

It is difficult to measure how many enemy deaths American armed forces have inflicted. Americans and their allies typically cause 10 to 20 times more combat casualties than American forces suffer. Estimates of Iraqi soldiers killed in the Gulf War range from 1,500 to 100,000. The lowest figure would still be 10 times the number of Americans killed in the war. Approximately 850,000 Vietcong died in the Vietnam War, 18 times the 47,000 U.S. dead. More than 600,000 North Korean and 1 million Chinese fighters died in the Korean War, almost 50 times the 33,000 American dead. In World War II, 3,250,000 German and 1,507,000 Japanese soldiers, sailors, and pilots were killed, 16 times the 291,000 American servicemen who were killed.[13]

How much does it cost the United States to maintain its armed forces?

Since 1975, America has spent between 3 and 6 percent of its gross domestic product on national defense, or approximately 15 to 30 percent of each year's federal budget. In the first years of the twenty-first century, this meant spending roughly $350 billion per year. In comparison, annual spending for other programs included roughly $15 billion on state and international assistance and $60 billion on education. From 1940 to 1996 (a period that includes several cycles of war and peace, including the arms race of the cold war), America spent $16.23 trillion on the military ($5.82 trillion of that on nuclear weapons), versus $1.70 trillion on health care and $1.24 trillion on international affairs.[14]

How much does war cost?

The cost of the Gulf War was approximately $76 billion.* Vietnam cost $500 billion; the Korean War, $336 billion; and World War II, almost $3 trillion. Put another way, the Gulf War cost

---

*All dollar amounts are in 2002 dollars. Each war's per-person cost is based on the total U.S. population at the peak of the war.

each person in the United States $306; Vietnam, $2,204 per person; Korea, $2,266 per person; and World War II, $20,388 per person. At its outset, estimates for the cost of the Iraqi War were $50 to $140 billion, and an additional $75 to $500 billion for occupation and peacekeeping, or from $444 to $2,274 per person.[15]

How big is the military industry in the United States?

Besides the 1.4 million active duty personnel, the military employs 627,000 civilians. The defense industry employs another 3 million. In total, the military and its supporting manufacturing base employs 3.5 percent of the U.S. labor force. In 2002, the Department of Defense spent $170.8 billion with military contractors such as Boeing and Lockheed Martin.[16]

How has the size of the industry changed over time?

The 2003 level of 3.5 percent of the labor force is historically low. In 1987, toward the end of the cold war, defense (including the military) made up 5.7 percent of the U.S. labor market; in 1968, during Vietnam, 9.8 percent; in 1943, during World War II, 39 percent. After World War II, defense employment dropped to 4.5 percent, but jumped back to 11 percent in 1951 with the Korean War and the start of the cold war.[17]

Does the military industry help make defense spending decisions?

Yes. In 2000, defense lobbying groups spent approximately $60 million. Defense political action committees also contribute roughly $14 million per congressional election cycle. Defense aerospace, defense electronics, and miscellaneous defense are the 31st-, 44th-, and 46th-ranking industries, respectively.[18]

How many weapons does the U.S. military industry export each year?

In 2001, U.S. arms manufacturers exported $9.7 billion in

weapons worldwide. The United Kingdom was second in international exports with $4 billion. In addition, the United States made new sales of $12.1 billion. Russia was second with $5.8 billion. The United States is the world's largest arms manufacturer, supplying almost half of all the arms sold on the world market.[19]

What kinds of arms does the United States export?

In 2002, U.S. manufacturers planned to export arms including Cobra and Apache attack helicopters, Black Hawk helicopters, KC-135A Stratotanker air-to-air tanker/transport aircraft, Hellfire and Hellfire II air-to-surface antiarmor missiles, Sidewinder air-to-air missiles, TOW 2A and 2B missiles, M-16 rifles, M-60 machine guns, grenade launchers, MK-82 (500 lb.) and MK-83 (1,000 lb.) bombs, Sentinel radar systems, GBU-12 Paveway series laser-guided bombs, standard assault amphibious personnel vehicles, assault amphibious command vehicles, and CBU-97 sensor fused weapon antitank cluster bombs.[20]

How many of the weapons U.S. companies export go to developing countries?

Approximately half. From 1994 to 2001, the United States exported $131 billion in arms, with $59 billion going to developing nations. The United States is the leading exporter to developing countries, with Russia and France second and third.[21]

How do American arms exports affect the American people?

Arms exports are an important source of American jobs and help maintain U.S. military manufacturing capacity. They also have some negative consequences. When American weapons are used in a conflict—for example, by Israel against the Palestinians—America is also blamed for the attacks. U.S. forces regularly find themselves up against sophisticated weaponry of American origin, which is harder to defend against.[22]

How dangerous is war for civilians?

Very dangerous. Between 1900 and 1990, 43 million soldiers died in wars. During the same period, 62 million civilians were killed. More than 34 million civilians died in World War II. One million died in North Korea. Hundreds of thousands were killed in South Korea, and 200,000 to 400,000 in Vietnam. In the wars of the 1990s, civilian deaths constituted between 75 and 90 percent of all war deaths.[23]

What is the civilian experience in war?

They are shot, bombed, raped, starved, and driven from their homes. During World War II, 135,000 civilians died in two days in the firebombing of Dresden. A week later, in Pforzheim, Germany, 17,800 people were killed in 22 minutes. In Russia, after the three-year battle of Leningrad, only 600,000 civilians remained in a city that had held a population of 2.5 million. One million were evacuated, 100,000 were conscripted into the Red Army, and 800,000 died. In April 2003, during the Iraqi War, half of the 1.3 million civilians in Basra, Iraq, were trapped for days without food and water in temperatures in excess of 100 degrees.[24]

How many refugees are there?

In 2001, 40 million people were displaced from their homes because of armed conflict or human rights violations. Refugees have been a concern throughout the twentieth century. Five million Europeans were uprooted from 1919 to 1939. World War II displaced 40 million non-Germans in Europe, and 13 million Germans were expelled from countries in Eastern Europe. Approximately 2.5 million of the 4.4 million people in Bosnia and Herzegovina were driven from their homes during that region's war in the early 1990s. More than 2 million Rwandans left their country in 1994. In 2001, 200,000 people were driven from Afghanistan to Pakistan. In early 2003, 45,000 Liberians were displaced from their homes.[25]

What are the consequences of becoming a refugee?

Refugees have very high mortality rates, due primarily to malnutrition and infectious disease. Rwandan refugees in Zaire in 1994 had a death rate 25 to 50 times higher than pre-war Rwandans. Iraqi Kurdish refugees in Turkey in 1991 had a death rate 18 times higher than usual.[26]

How does war affect children?

More than 2 million children were killed in wars during the 1990s. Three times that number were disabled or seriously injured. Twenty million children were displaced from their homes in 2001. Many were forced into prostitution. A large percentage of those will contract AIDS. Children born to mothers who are raped or forced into prostitution often become outcasts.[27]

How many child soldiers are there?

More than 300,000 worldwide. Soldiers are sometimes recruited at age 10 and younger. The youngest carry heavy packs, or sweep roads with brooms and branches to test for landmines. When children are hostile, the opposing army is more likely to consider every civilian a potential enemy.[28]

Why do children join armies?

They are often forced to. Some are given alcohol or drugs, or exposed to atrocities, to desensitize them to violence. Some join to help feed or protect their families. Some are offered up by their parents in exchange for protection. Children can be fearless because they lack a clear concept of death.[29]

How can war affect women?

Women often take on larger economic roles in wartime. They must find ways to compensate for their husband's military deployment or unemployment. Those in war zones must search for food, water, medicine, and fuel despite shortages. Some women in war zones are forced into prostitution to provide for their family. Famine and stress cause increased stillbirth and early infant death. AIDS risk increases for many women in war, from prostitution, husbands who return from military duty with HIV, or rape.[30]

What is genocide?

Genocide is any number of acts committed with intent to destroy, in whole or in part, a national, ethnic, racial, or religious group, according to the United Nations. Others include political and social groups in the definition, making genocide more broadly the annihilation of difference. Genocidal campaigns have become more frequent since World War I. Modern industrial weapons have made mass killings easier to commit.[31]

How many genocides have occurred since World War I?

Dozens. The most devastating include those in the Soviet Union, where approximately 20 million were killed during Stalin's Great Terror (1930s); Nazi Germany, where 6 million Jews were killed in concentration camps along with 5 million or more Gypsies, Jehovah's Witnesses, and other "enemies of the German state" (1937–1945); Cambodia, where 1.7 million of the country's 7 million people were killed as a result of the actions of the Khmer Rouge (1975–1979); Iraq, where 50,000 Kurds were killed during the ethnic cleansing of Anfal in 1987; Bosnia, where 310,000 Muslims were killed (1992–1995); and Rwanda, where more than 1 million Tutsis and moderate Hutus were slaughtered over ten weeks in 1994.[32]

Chapter 2

ENLISTMENT

How is the U.S. military organized?

The U.S. military is run by the Department of Defense. It oversees the Departments of the Army, Navy, and Air Force, which are responsible for land, sea, and air fighting respectively. The Marine Corps is a branch of the Department of the Navy; it is available for operations on both water and land, such as shoreline fighting. The Marine Corps is also a "force in readiness," often the first branch to enter a fight. The Coast Guard is part of the military only in wartime; otherwise it is run by the Department of Homeland Security.

Those in the Army are called soldiers; in the Navy, sailors; in the Air Force, airmen; and in the Marine Corps, Marines. All branches have Reserve units, available for deployment in wartime. The Army and Air Force also have National Guards. The branches compete for funding, and have their own training methods, battle strategies, and cultures.[1]

How is the U.S. military used to fight wars?

The president is the commander in chief of the U.S. military. He gives orders to the secretary of defense, a civilian, who in turn gives orders to the unified combatant commander responsible for the area where the war will be fought. Unified Combatant Command, which commands troops in battle, is not organized by service branch. Each unified commander is responsible for a large part of the world, such as Europe or South America, or a broad area of expertise, such as transportation or strategy.

The Army, Navy, and Air Force each have a civilian secretary and a military chief of staff. The highest military office in the Marines is commandant. The four top military leaders make up the Office of the Joint Chiefs of Staff, which also includes a chairman and vice chairman, who may come from any branch. These six officers advise the president on military affairs, but have no command power.[2]

Why do most people join the military?

Most people join the U.S. armed services to fund their education (33 percent of men, 33 percent of women in 1008) or for job training (34 percent, 31 percent).[3]

What is the average recruit like?

Of the more than 100,000 men and women who joined the Army in 2002, 8 percent had prior military service. About 80 percent were men. About 65 percent were white, 18 percent black, 13 percent Hispanic, and 5 percent other races, including Asian and Pacific Islander. The average age was 21.1 years, with 12.1 years of education. Eighty-four percent were single.[4]

What is the purpose of military training and discipline?

The training goal is to develop a combat-ready force that is physically and psychologically prepared to fight and survive. Training and discipline make it easier for you to engage in combat and kill. You will be far more willing and able to kill when a strong, respected leader commands you to, and when a group of soldiers with whom you have close bonds are also fighting and killing beside you. That is why the military emphasizes leadership, discipline, and strong bonds within your unit.[5]

What will happen to me at boot camp?

The military will exert total control over your life. You will be stripped of the things that marked you as a civilian. You will get a standard military haircut and a uniform to reduce individuality and build unit identity. You may be insulted and forced to fail in order to break down your pride and capacity to resist authority. You may be made to do tasks at which you are unskilled, and punished when you fail at them. You will live communally, without privacy or luxury, and participate in activities collectively with your platoon. You will undergo constant strenuous physical and psychological conditioning. Aggressiveness will be emphasized. You will be rewarded for success at a few military tasks. A hierarchy will form based on your relative success rates. You will be required to rely on your teammates to succeed.

After basic training and advanced training you will be expected to operate without supervision. You will learn to use weapons and train for combat. You will get in shape to meet fitness standards. You will learn teamwork, military values, and history. You will be expected to operate under stress. At the end of basic training, you will be tested with an extended field exercise. Upon completing it, you will attend a graduation ceremony.[6]

Will I be injured during basic training?

You may strain a muscle or receive a repetitive stress injury like a stress fracture. In one eight-week study of basic training, 380 out of a class of 1,357 recruits suffered an injury.[7]

How much will I have to march?

It depends on your branch of the military. If you are in the Army, for the first two weeks, you will march three miles per day with your helmet and weapon. Weeks three through five, you will march between four and five miles per day with helmet, weapon, and a 10-pound rucksack. Weeks six through eight, you will march six miles per day with helmet, weapon, and a 20-pound rucksack.[8]

Will I be hazed?

Recruits are frequently humiliated. They are made to carry out demeaning tasks. All four service branches have put regulations in place restricting abuse toward recruits.[9]

How many recruits wash out of basic training?

In 2001, 12 percent of Marine Corps recruits dropped out, as did 14 percent in the Army and Navy, and 7 percent in the Air Force.[10]

Why do most recruits wash out?

For medical reasons, including injuries and previously undisclosed physical or mental conditions.[11]

How does the military condition me to fight and kill?

It will prepare you for combat through constant target practice and combat simulations that include using human-shaped targets.[12]

What if I am asked to do something I consider immoral?

The military will condition you to act based on your orders, not on your conscience. However, if you believe an order to be unlawful, you must refuse to carry it out.[13]

What factors would make me ineligible to enlist?

If you are under age 17, over 35, are not a U.S. citizen or a lawful permanent resident, have a felony conviction, are married and have more than two dependent children under age 18, are unmarried and have any dependent children, or score below the tenth percentile on the Armed Forces Qualification

Test, you are ineligible for military service. You can apply for a waiver.[14]

What medical defects will keep me out of the military?

Anything that renders you physically unable to serve. Some specific ailments include contagious diseases, chronic diarrhea, hepatitis, anemia, diabetes, night blindness, male body fat of more than 24 percent for ages 17 to 20 or more than 26 percent for ages 21 to 27, female body fat of more than 30 percent for ages 17 to 20 or more than 32 percent for ages 21 to 27, asthma, epilepsy, sleepwalking, herpes, color blindness, narcolepsy, arthritis, exhibitionism, voyeurism, psychotic disorders, anxiety attacks, suicidal tendencies, eating disorders, and stuttering. Also, braces and other orthodonture except retainers, frequent encounters with law enforcement, and inappropriate tattoos, such as any on your face.[15]

How have people avoided military service in the past?

During the Vietnam War, 5,276,000 men were granted physical, mental, psychiatric, or moral exemptions, versus 2,215,000 who were drafted and served in the military. The most common techniques of dodging the draft in the Vietnam War were: having a sympathetic doctor write a letter on your behalf listing allergies, drug addictions, and personality disorders; losing or gaining an extreme amount of weight; getting every question on the intelligence test wrong; inhaling enough dust to give yourself an asthma attack; getting braces; depriving yourself of sleep for days; borrowing thick glasses and faking poor vision; listening to loud sounds to damage your hearing; claiming homosexuality; coming to your examination intoxicated; chopping off a thumb joint; staring at the sun to partially blind yourself; pinpricking your arms to fake heroin needle scars; shooting yourself in the foot. Many Vietnam-era deferments and exemptions were granted to conscientious objectors (171,700), students

14

(371,000), ministers (48,000), teachers, engineers, and farmers (435,000), as well as others who were married, had a child, or otherwise qualified for a hardship deferment (2,420,000). Of the 209,517 who were accused of criminally evading the draft, 4,000 went to prison and 4,750 were given probation.[16]

Can I sign up for a job that will keep me out of combat?

No. Every job in the military carries the possibility of being sent to the front lines. When you enlist, you will take an aptitude test. Once it has been determined what jobs you are best suited for, you may be given your choice between them. Even if you choose an administrative or logistics position, you will still be given combat training. If you are needed, you will be deployed to a combat zone, where you will be expected to kill enemy soldiers (unless you are a medic or a chaplain) and to protect your comrades' lives in battle.[17]

What are the most dangerous military jobs?

Infantry positions in the Army and Marines. These are the units that directly engage the enemy in ground combat. Though they only account for 10 to 30 percent of the troops in a war, infantry can suffer as many as 80 percent of the casualties. John Ellis writes in *The Sharp End: The Fighting Man in World War II* that "In Tunisia, the infantry, armor, and field artillery, between a quarter and a third of the total Army strength, accounted for 80.2 percent of the total casualties. In northwest Europe, it has been estimated, these formations sustained 81 percent of the total battle casualties. The infantry, as usual, were particularly hard hit. Though they represented only 20.5 percent of the total Army strength, they accounted for 66.7 percent of the total battle casualties. Armored divisions made up another 10.6 percent and airborne units 3.7 percent." You are roughly ten times more likely to die in an infantry position than you are in a non-infantry role.[18]

What qualities does the military look for in those who join elite units?

To volunteer for Army Special Forces, you must be male, be a high school graduate or have a GED, achieve minimum scores on intelligence and physical tests, be able to swim 50 meters in full uniform, have parachute training, and qualify for security clearance. To volunteer for Navy SEALs, you must pass a physical and an intelligence test, be a male between 18 and 28, have little or no history of criminal behavior, and volunteer for diving duty. Traditionally, it has been impossible to enlist directly in special operations forces. Applicants must have risen to a certain rank in their service branch before they can be considered. Other attributes for evaluating candidate suitability include motivation, trustworthiness, accountability, maturity, stability, judgment, decisiveness, and teamwork.[19]

Why is it hard to join elite units?

Early 1960s research into special forces by the U.S. Army Personnel Research Office identified eight basic conditions that challenge the special forces officer: extreme fatigue, the necessity of performing in an unstructured situation, conflict situations, the need to accept training as real combat, performance with no knowledge of personal progress, inability to leave the course voluntarily, the necessity for teamwork, and the need to observe and retain certain military information. The research also identified 10 reactions that appeared to have potential for differentiating the poor from the adequate fighter: malingering, lack of social responsibility, an attitude of martyrdom, unauthorized withdrawal, hostility, fear of injury, uneasiness with the unknown, psychotic-like reactions, failure to assume the combat role, and inability to follow instructions.[20]

How hard is it to join an elite unit?

Because of more rigorous prescreening, approximately half of today's special forces candidates make it through assessment and selection, while only 29 percent did in the past. If you meet the special forces prerequisites you will have to complete lengthy, multiphase training. In the first phase, assessment and selection, you will be placed under extreme levels of physical and mental stress, and deprived of sleep, food, and water. In later phases, you will have to learn skills such as survival, navigation, tactics, a foreign language, and an occupational skill such as leadership, weapons, engineering, medicine, or communications.

Prospective Navy SEALs are subjected to intense pain and suffering. Ranger School, for Army Rangers, is strenuous and stressful, allowing its soldiers so little sleep that they may hallucinate. Many soldiers lose twenty pounds in sixty days.[21]

What is the median income of those who enlist?

The average new recruit receives about $13,000 in base pay in the first year. Taking into account food and housing allowances, as well as the tax advantages of military service, the "regular military compensation" of the average new recruit is approximately $24,000 per year. The median military household income in 2001 was $33,226. Salary growth is slower in the military than for the average civilian male with some college education.[22]

How many military personnel are on food stamps?

About 4,200 military families were receiving food stamps in 2001.[23]

How often do people reenlist?

The average enlistee stays in the military for about seven years, up from less than two years in 1973. In 2000, 25 percent of first-term Marine Corps enlistees reenlisted or extended their service, as did 38 percent of those in the Army, 44 percent in the Navy, and 42 percent in the Air Force. In 2002, 58 percent of the military, including 43 percent of the lowest-rank enlistees, considered themselves likely to reenlist. Forty-six percent of Marines were likely to reenlist, compared with 58 percent of the Army, 60 percent of the Navy, and 63 percent of the Air Force.[24]

How long is the typical reenlistment term?

Four to five years. Reenlistment terms are longer in the Navy. In all branches, shorter extensions of service, often one year or less, are also available.[25]

How often will I get leave?

You will have 30 days of leave a year, accumulated at a rate of 2.5 days every month. You are encouraged to take at least two weeks at a time. In addition, you may be granted a pass for up to 72 hours, or even 96 hours in special cases. You can be denied leave based on military necessity.[26]

How long do I have to serve before I get a pension?

You must serve 20 years to receive a military pension. After 15 years of service you can choose a $30,000 bonus in exchange for a lower pension after you retire.[27]

Where will I live?

Thirty-five percent of military families and 82 percent of single and unaccompanied military personnel lived in military housing in 1995. In the same year, the average military house was 33 years old and in need of extensive repair. Sixty-four percent were classified as "unsuitable." In 2000, the "basic allowance for housing" was increased to make it easier for those in the military to afford private homes.[28]

Can my spouse work on my base if he or she is not in the military?

Yes, and he or she will be given preference by military employers. Your spouse must be qualified for the position. He or she will be given preference once per permanent relocation.[29]

If I am a man in the military, is my wife likely to work?

Military wives, compared to civilian wives, are less likely to work. They work fewer hours when they do work. They make an average of $10,241 per year, versus $15,884 for the civilian wives. The likelihood that your wife will work declines as you spend more time in the service.[30]

If I stay in the military, how often will I move?

You will probably move about every two years. One third of military members make permanent change of station (PCS) moves each year. Your tours of duty will grow longer as your rank increases. Fifty-seven percent of lowest-ranking enlistees make PCS moves after less than one year, compared with only 9 percent of highest-ranking officers. Twenty-eight percent of Marines move after less than one year. Twenty-one percent of Army and Navy personnel and 13 percent of Air Force members do.[31]

Will I be unhappy to move?

Those who move frequently are the least satisfied with the military. They report problems with housing, employment for the nonmilitary spouse, and cost of living.[32]

Will my family come with me?

Maybe not. Sixteen percent of enlistees are unaccompanied by their spouses. Nine percent of those married with dependent children are unaccompanied by their families. Fifty-one percent of single parents are unaccompanied by their dependent children. Unaccompanied military personnel are about 10 percent less satisfied with their lives and jobs, and are about 10 percent more likely to leave military service before retirement age.[33]

How will my family be affected by frequent moves and my absence?

If you are deployed, especially in wartime, your spouse may experience cycles of depression. Your children may be depressed, aggressive, or overly dependent. If they are young, your children may have nightmares and cry frequently, and be rebellious or shy. Family troubles due to your deployment may last as long as a year after reunion.[34]

Will I be more likely to divorce?

If you are in a battle, even a short one, you will more likely divorce. In 2001, 1.6 percent of active duty officers and 2.8 percent of active duty enlistees divorced. Selected Reserve officers and enlistees had 3.1 percent and 2.7 percent divorce rates, respectively, in the same period. In the year 2000, .41 percent of Americans divorced, but that number includes the young and very old. Thus, while the figures are not directly comparable, it appears the military has a higher divorce rate.[35]

Will I be more likely to abuse my spouse?

Yes. One Army survey of 55,000 soldiers at 47 bases showed that one of every three families has suffered some kind of domestic violence, from slapping to murder. This is twice the rate found in similar groups of civilians. The Pentagon has disclosed that an average of one child or spouse dies each week at the hands of a relative in the military.[36]

What is the family background of the average recruit?

In 1999, 69 percent of active duty recruits came from a two-parent home, compared with 71 percent of same-age civilians. Among the recruits' parents, 53 percent of their fathers and 49 percent of their mothers had at least some college education, compared with 56 and 50 percent of civilian fathers and mothers.[37]

What percentage of the U.S. military is minority?

Of the active military's 1.4 million people, 490,000, or 35 percent, are minorities. Twenty percent are black, 8 percent are Hispanic, 4 percent are Asian or Pacific Islander, and 1 percent is Native American or Alaska Native. This compares to the general population's 12 percent black, 13 percent Hispanic, 4 percent Asian or Pacific Islander, and .1 percent Native American or Alaska Native. In the Army, half of all enlisted women are black; 38 percent are white. Hispanic and Asian representation is increasing quickly. There are 37,401 foreign nationals serving in the military.[38]

Is there racism in the military?

Yes. Blacks are twice as likely as whites to perceive racial discrimination in the military, though a majority of black soldiers say race relations are better in the military than in civilian life. Black soldiers are two times more likely to be jailed than white soldiers —but black civilians are six times more likely to be jailed than whites. Black officers are less likely than whites to be promoted into the middle ranks, but are more likely to remain between promotions. The officer corps is not disproportionately white. The military emphasizes that divisions of any kind increase deaths in wartime. The institutional culture prevents most outright racism.[39]

Are blacks more committed to the military than whites?

Yes. Black enlistees are 50 percent more likely than whites not to leave during their first tour, and 50 percent more likely than whites to reenlist after it. Fifty percent of qualified black youth join the military, compared to 16 percent of qualified whites.[40]

Are minorities forced into the most dangerous jobs?

No. Many blacks think of the military as a career. They look for jobs with greater civilian transferability. They are two and a half times more likely than whites to take administrative and support jobs. Whites are 50 percent more likely to serve in the infantry and on gun crews. They are also more likely to serve in special operations forces. Hispanics, a rapidly growing population in the military, tend to take dangerous infantry jobs.[41]

Are women allowed to go into combat?

Yes. Women cannot join certain Army ground combat specialties to include infantry, armor, and field artillery. However, they can join Air Defense Artillery. They can also find themselves assigned to infantry, armor, and field artillery units in staff and support positions requiring such specialties as military intelligence, transportation, signal, and quartermaster. They also join combat-support units that bring them in contact with the enemy. These include aviation, engineers, and military police units. Women are given the same combat training as men, though Marine basic training units are segregated by gender. As of 1993 women can fly combat aircraft in the Air Force and Navy. During the 2003 Iraqi War, women flew combat missions in support of Marine and Army infantry units. They can be Army paratroopers. They can be assigned to all navy vessels except submarines and those too small to provide adequate privacy. While most special operations units are closed to women, they can be assigned to psychological operations and civil affairs units, which are part of U.S. Special Operations Command.[42]

Are women more attracted to men in the military?

Sometimes. During World War II, in the United States, "Victory Girls" had sex with servicemen as their "patriotic duty." In war-torn, poverty-stricken countries, women are often attracted to servicemen for the money and goods they can obtain.[43]

Are men less attracted to the women in the military?

Perhaps. Forty-two percent of female military personnel are married, versus 60 percent of the adult U.S. population. Fifty-three percent of military men are married.[44]

How common is pregnancy?

About 5 percent of women in the military are pregnant at any given time, compared to 11 percent of civilian women. In some war-fighting divisions, which have younger-than-average women, 10 percent are pregnant at any time.[45]

What happens if I get pregnant?

You are "nondeployable." You cannot be sent on missions and field exercises. If you are on deployment, you will be withdrawn. Navy women are immediately transferred to shore duty. Men in your regiment might have to take on extra work. You will receive a 42-day maternity leave.[46]

Will I stay in the military after my pregnancy?

Probably. About one third of women bear their children and stay, one third have an abortion and stay, and one third bear their children and leave, according to unofficial estimates.[47]

Is there sexism in the military?

There are sexual double standards. Men tend to believe that women belong in the military, but not in jobs for which they are physically unfit. A minority of men and women believe the opposite sex is given more of the "dirty work." Women officers are underrepresented in the higher ranks. Reasons given by male officers for this difference include perceived female physical and mental incapability, the combat exclusion that keeps women from career-enhancing assignments, and a fear of sexual harassment accusations that prevents male superiors from establishing the close working relationships that lead to promotion. Female officers also name the interference of assignments with family life.[48]

Should I be concerned about being raped or sexually harassed in the military?

Six percent of military women and less than 1 percent of men reported rape or attempted rape in 1995. Seventy-eight percent of women and 38 percent of men reported sexual harassment. The Marines had the highest rate of women reporting sexual harassment and rape: 86 percent and 9 percent, respectively. The Air Force had the lowest, 74 percent and 4 percent. Junior enlistees and blacks were more likely to be harassed than senior officers and whites. Less than 7 percent of military women reported being harassed by civilians.[49]

If I am raped or sexually harassed, will my complaint be taken seriously?

Not always. In a 1995 survey, 10 percent of military women said they were encouraged to drop their complaint, 23 percent said it was not taken seriously, 12 percent said their supervisor was hostile, and 15 percent said no action was taken on their claim.[50]

If I am homosexual, will I be able to get into the military?

Yes, as long as you do not tell the military. Sexual orientation is considered a personal and private matter. Homosexual orientation is not a bar to service entry or continued service unless manifested by homosexual activity. You will not be asked about your sexual orientation. If you say that you are homosexual, or anyone presents evidence that you are, you will be denied entry into the military.[51]

How common is homosexuality in the military?

Some say the military has a higher percentage of homosexuals than the general population. No exact figures exist, but estimates range as high as 12 percent. In the Navy, "the homosexual presence on aircraft carriers is so pervasive that social life on the huge ships . . . has included gay newspapers and clandestine gay discos." From 1994 to 2002, the Army discharged 2,939 people for homosexuality, the Navy discharged 2,804, the Air Force discharged 2,297, and the Marines discharged 754.[52]

Is there homophobia in the military?

Yes, though personal contact with homosexuals decreases it slightly. In the Army, 16 percent of men and 40 percent of women who didn't know of a homosexual in their unit were in favor of allowing homosexuals in the military. Twenty-two percent of men and 52 percent of women who did know of a homosexual in their unit were in favor of it.[53]

Will someone of the same sex pursue me?

In a 1992 Army study, 6 percent of men and 17 percent of women felt someone had made a homosexual advance toward them.[54]

Am I guaranteed a career in the military?

Not necessarily. The size of the military is subject to the budgetary decisions of Congress and the president. It has historically been reduced in peacetime. The 1990s, with the end of the cold war, saw a military drawdown of more than a third. Much of this force reduction was accomplished willingly through early-retirement incentives. After the reduction, many military personnel worried about their job security. They were deployed more frequently and with less warning, causing additional stress. Eighteen months after returning from the Gulf War, 27 percent of surveyed troops were concerned about being able to stay on in the military because of downsizing, and 36 percent were concerned about their career and chances for promotion.[55]

Will I have career friendships?

It will be difficult. Rotation will limit the length of your friendships, and make you wary of becoming close to your current friends. When your friendships last they will often be intense ones, because military life forces you to rely heavily on others and because work and friendship are so thoroughly mixed.[56]

Will the skills I learn in the military be useful in civilian life?

It depends on your occupational specialty. One third to one half of veterans acquire skills such as foreign languages, equipment repair, communications, and medicine that are transferable to civilian work. "Muddy boots" jobs tend not to transfer. The Army and the Marines provide fewer of its personnel with transferable skills than do the Navy and Air Force.[57]

What kind of job will I take after my service?

A study of the British military found that 40 percent of junior military men pursued civilian careers with similarities to the military, such as prison guard, police officer, or others in the defense and security industries.[58]

What will it be like to retire?

Retiring from the military after 20 or more years can be difficult. Independence replaces rules and support systems. Some veterans value this freedom, but others find it difficult. Without a uniform, you may feel your status is eliminated. This will be especially troubling if you are an aggressive, independent personality who held leadership positions. You may miss the hierarchy that valued your devotion. You may seek a job in another highly structured environment.[59]

Will I stay in touch with my military friends after I retire?

You will try. Both your post-retirement decline in income and the fact that most civilians already have friends will make you more likely to seek out your military friends. You may move to a community with a large military retiree population, near a military post, where your status will be recognized. If your military friends live elsewhere, you will be able to meet others with similar experiences.[60]

Chapter 3

LIFE IN WAR

What will it be like if my unit is one of the first deployed?

It will be stressful. You may be ahead of your supply chain. You may sleep in overcrowded facilities, with little time to yourself. Without sports or recreation equipment, you will be forced to improvise. In the Gulf War, the first troops built sports equipment out of bars, bags of sand, and cement. Some passed the time by arranging and betting on scorpion races. As other troops and supplies arrive, your quality of life will improve.[1]

Do I get paid more for time in combat?

Yes. You receive a $150 per month bonus. Your earnings for that month are tax free.[2]

What will I eat?

It will depend on what you are supposed to do that day. If you have a day of hard work ahead, you will be given a carbohydrate-rich meal. If your mission requires peak cognitive ability, you will receive protein. You may be given food rich in carbohydrates and low in protein to make you tired if you need to sleep during irregular hours. A typical meal ready to eat (MRE) or self-heating individual meal module (SHIMM) might include a

Salisbury steak, bread, and a specially formulated chocolate bar that is designed not to melt in hot climates. In a cold environment, you will get 5 to 10 percent more calories than your regular ration. In hot climates you will probably not be as hungry, but will also need to eat more—approximately 1 percent more calories for every two degrees above 86 degrees Fahrenheit.[3]

What if I am separated from my unit and need food?

For survival, you should carry a cut-down ration in your pants cargo pocket, and one tube of bouillon cubes in the first aid pouch on your suspenders and pistol belt. One bouillon cube dissolved in one canteen of water will provide energy for one or two days. If that runs out, you may be able to steal food from farms, villages, or camps. However, farms may have dogs or chickens, which can be expected to react with alarm at your approach. Stealing food from villages or camps is difficult. Food, especially in wartime, is usually safeguarded against theft.[4]

Will I get dehydrated?

If you are not careful, you can become dehydrated without feeling thirsty. Dehydration renders your blood less able to carry oxygen to your brain and muscles. It results in instant battle fatigue. You need to minimize the amount of water you lose. Keep your clothing closed to trap sweat next to your skin. You lose one pint of water per day through normal breathing, so keep your mouth closed and breathe through your nose. A cloth across your mouth and nose will reduce water loss. Water is a precious commodity during wartime.[5]

How will I go to the bathroom?

A central latrine will be established for multiple camps. One latrine will usually serve the needs of three to four shelters or a unit of platoon size (about 40 people).[6]

Will I be constipated?

Possibly. Military rations were engineered to keep you from needing to defecate more often than once every three days. However, current military menus are often augmented with fresh fruit, vegetables, and bread to provide roughage and nutrients.[7]

What if I have to move my bowels immediately?

An empty ration box, lined with a trash bag, can suffice. Full bags can be sealed, left in the box, and then hauled to the rear.[8]

How often will I be able to shower or bathe?

You should be able to shower or take a bath at least once every week. If showers or baths are not available, use a washcloth to wash daily.[9]

Will I have privacy in the shower?

Maybe not. If you're uncomfortable showering in front of others, bring a lightweight nylon swimsuit.[10]

How else should I maintain my personal hygiene during a war?

Change your socks as often as you need to in order to keep your feet dry. Use foot powder as a dry rub to clean your feet. Men should shave at night so the facial oils stripped during shaving will be replenished overnight. It is important to brush your teeth daily. If a toothbrush is not available, chew the end of a twig into a makeshift brush. If a twig is not available, use salt on a fingertip.[11]

What happens if I get my period?

Make sure to bring a supply of feminine hygiene products adequate for a prolonged period of time. You may not be able to get more.[12]

What will I do when I am not fighting?

In a full deployment with a stable front, you will have access to exercise and athletic equipment. You can also read or listen to music.[13]

Will the military make me as comfortable as possible?

No. "It is best for the soldier not to be too comfortable," says one field manual. The military would rather have you in a state of alert. You will be expected to be physically and psychologically ready to fight.[14]

Will I be able to watch television?

Probably. Morale is important to the cohesion of a fighting unit. If a combat front is stabilized you will probably have the chance to watch movies, TV shows, and sports in a communal recreation building or tent.[15]

Should I believe what I see on TV about the war?

Not necessarily. The presence of the media in the modern battle environment makes it hard to hide significant troop action. However, it also presents an opportunity to provide misinformation. In the Gulf War, U.S. military leaders told the media that the main attack on Iraq was likely to be an amphibious assault on its eastern border with Kuwait. The media repeated this. News teams focused their efforts on covering the troop buildup in that area. The enemy did the same and was unprepared when the U.S.-led attack streamed into Iraq from the Saudi Arabian border in the west.[16]

Can I send and receive letters during war?

Yes. The maintenance of mail service is important to troop morale. The military works to establish service as soon as conditions stabilize along a front. Outbound mail is free.[17]

Can I call home?

You may be able to make phone calls from telephones set up by the military, but you will probably have to wait in a long line.[18]

Will I have access to a computer with email service?

Probably, though you will face stiff competition from your comrades to use it.[19]

Will I make friends during combat?

You will have a comrade whom you take care of and who takes care of you. His loyalty will be to you, not to the larger group. He may stay with you if you are wounded, even though he is supposed to continue the attack.[20]

Will I be bored?

At times, though combat deployment has changed greatly in the past 20 years. A common description of wartime has been "waiting and boredom punctuated by brief periods of terror." This reflects a style of warfare that included stable fronts, conventional weaponry, and defined firefights that had a start and an end. In the Gulf War, the state of the troops was marked by constant agitation and stress due to the close quarters, unfamiliar terrain, potential for use of chemical weapons, and the uncertainty of the mission and of the support they would receive back home.[21]

Will I become more religious?

Probably. War stimulates a new or stronger need for religious faith. Given the prevalence of violence, and the seeming randomness of who lives and dies, many in war find themselves drawn to the idea of a higher power.[22]

Will I become superstitious?

Probably. Having superstitions in wartime can reduce your anxiety. If you have control over something (a talisman, an article of clothing) that you believe can help you in an uncontrollable and dangerous environment, it can be comforting. In an article on luck in wartime, one Vietnam veteran explained, "Superstition is as common on the battlefield as foxholes and shell casings." The most common superstition is belief in a lucky charm, like a coin, medal, or family heirloom.[23]

Will I think about sex?

Yes, all the time, especially if you are not in a forward deployment. If you are on the front lines, under direct and extreme stress, you may think about it less. The longer you are away from home, the more promiscuous you may be. The average American serviceman serving in Europe in World War II had sex with 25 women in the last year of the war.[24]

Can I have consensual sex with others in the military?

Yes, though it is frowned on because it might distract from your unit's mission. Adulterous sex is subject to court-martial, as is nonconsensual sex and sex with minors. Sex between enlisted personnel and officers may be subject to court-martial under the rules against fraternization. Sex between any two people with a duty relationship that might create the appearance of favoritism is prohibited.[25]

Will I be able to meet local members of the opposite sex?

Not necessarily. In Muslim nations especially, the military may keep you from interacting with members of the opposite sex. Almost 70 percent of those deployed to Saudi Arabia before the Gulf War said that not having the opposite sex around caused them "quite a bit" of or "extreme" stress. It was the number one reported source of stress.[26]

Will I visit prostitutes?

Solicitation of prostitutes by U.S. military personnel is a fact of life in many countries. Prostitution is a source of income in and around military bases. Large sex industries formed in Japan, South Korea, Vietnam, and elsewhere in Asia when U.S. troops were stationed there. Almost 27,000 prostitutes still operate around bases in South Korea. South Vietnam had between 300,000 and 500,000 prostitutes during the war. The average Green Beret had sex with 25 Vietnamese prostitutes. During the Gulf War, few U.S. servicemembers visited prostitutes, since there was no prostitution system in place and the conflict was brief. However, ships returning from the Gulf War often made a "sex stop" in Thailand.[27]

Will I lose interest in sex?

Maybe, if you are scared before combat. Twenty-two percent of those surveyed before combat in the Gulf War reported moderate to extreme discomfort due to loss of interest in sex. Seventy percent reported full interest in sex. After combat, 7 percent reported moderate to extreme discomfort due to loss of sex drive. Eighty-six percent reported full interest.[28]

Will I be able to drink alcohol during wartime?

Probably not. Officially, you may drink while off duty. However, your commander may decide that combat is such a constant threat that it justifies banning alcohol entirely.[29]

What if I get caught using drugs?

Under the Uniform Code of Military Justice, the maximum punishment for wrongful use of drugs is confinement for five years, dishonorable discharge, and forfeiture of all pay and allowances. If you are caught with less than 30 grams of marijuana, you can be confined for two years. For most drugs, if you had intent to distribute the drugs, it is fifteen years. If you are intoxicated on any substance while on duty, you can be punished with three months confinement and forfeiture of two-thirds of your pay for three months.[30]

Am I more likely to use drugs when I am deployed?

Drug use was a major problem for the military in Vietnam. Official reports show that as many as 35 percent of the troops smoked marijuana, with other observers putting the number closer to 75 percent. (The problem is not confined to combat. One Army authority said in 1971 that 50 to 70 percent of the men on base at Fort Bragg used marijuana.) Marijuana makes you incapacitated for duty for up to 12 to 36 hours. However, drug use in the Gulf War was dramatically reduced due to rigorous and random drug testing.[31]

How common is drug use in the military in general?

Drug use in the military is at a historical low. In 1980, close to 30 percent of those surveyed had used an illegal drug in the past thirty days. By 1998 that number had dropped to 3 percent, with only 6 percent saying they had used a drug in the past year, thanks in part to random drug testing. Thirty percent of the military smoked cigarettes in 1998, and 15 percent were heavy consumers of alcohol. Nineteen percent of men aged 18 to 24 used smokeless tobacco.[32]

What are my chances of sustaining a non-battle injury or contracting a disease?

Disease was once a greater threat to military forces than enemy fire. Injury and disease affected 67 percent of the deployed forces in World War II and 77 percent of those in Korea. Today, thanks to antibiotics and better training, rates have been lowered to approximately 15 percent in the Gulf War and 6 percent in Bosnia. The most common causes of non-battle injury in the American military are sports, falls, and motor vehicle accidents.[33]

Will I be vaccinated against local diseases before I am deployed?

Vaccines are part of a preventive medicine regimen before, during, and after deployment. You will be vaccinated against several common infectious diseases either during training or later. Before deployment, you will receive routine booster shots as well as any necessary vaccines. Before the Gulf War, U.S. Central Command issued guidance to vaccinate against meningococcus, typhoid, yellow fever, immune globulin, anthrax, and botulinum toxin.[34]

Are these inoculations safe?

Drugs that are used during combat do not have to pass normal trials. Pyridostigmine bromide (PB) was given in the Gulf War as a precaution against nerve gas attacks. The U.S. Food and Drug Administration permitted the military to use the drug although it was never tested. Those who took PB participated in the first large-scale use of the drug. Studies showed that one of the psychological stressors of the conflict was taking "untried, experimental drugs." Between 20 and 30 percent of those surveyed said they had not taken the PB tablets or had stopped after one administration.[35]

What diseases could I get?

Skin infections like ringworm are common in tropical climates. They were the most common cause of outpatient hospital visits in the Vietnam War. In one study, 65 percent of combat troops had "significant" skin infections. Water that is not properly treated can transmit diseases such as typhoid fever, bacillary dysentery, cholera, poliomyelitis, and common diarrhea. In some areas, water may also be the means of transmitting infectious hepatitis, schistosomiasis, and amoebic dysentery. Drinking clean water will help you stay free of disease. If the temperature outside exceeds 100 degrees Fahrenheit, the temperature of your water must be monitored. If the water temperature exceeds 92 degrees Fahrenheit, it should be changed, as bacteria will multiply. If you drink this water, you will get diarrhea.[36]

How can I avoid diarrhea?

Drink clean water. Avoid local water and food. You should change the water in your canteen every 24 hours. Water in trailers, if kept in the shade, will last up to five days. Local food and water sources, including ice, may be contaminated with pathogenic bacteria, parasites, and viruses to which you may have little or no natural immunity. Diarrheal diseases can temporarily incapacitate a high percentage of personnel. In the initial deployments of the Gulf War, more than 50 percent of the troops in some forward units reported an episode of acute diarrhea. The preparation of meals by foreign food handlers and use of locally catered meals contributed to this problem. For shipboard personnel, a major risk factor for diarrheal disease was eating in restaurants on shore leave.[37]

How can I avoid other infectious diseases?

Wear loose-fitting and untailored clothing on field operations. Tight-fitting clothing often tears or rips, allowing disease-carrying insects easy access to exposed parts of the body. Wear gloves to protect hands from insect bites. Gloves will also provide camouflage and aid in holding a weapon when it heats up from being fired.[38]

How will I sleep?

Sleep is as precious a resource as food or drink. Ideally, you will get at least 4 hours of uninterrupted sleep in each 24-hour period, and a total of 6 to 8 hours of sleep when smaller blocks of time are included. You may be ordered to take naps. Naps of even 15 to 30 minutes can be helpful, though 5-minute naps are not. You will be given earplugs.[39]

Where will I sleep?

Initially, you will likely be in a barracks. In the Gulf War, troops slept on cots inches apart from each other. Others slept in holes dug next to vehicles because cots had not arrived. You may eventually get your own tent.[40]

Will the fighting continue all night?

Yes. In fact, the U.S. military takes advantage of inhospitable conditions. As militaries around the world acquire more sophisticated radar and night-vision systems, more warfare takes place in darkness.[41]

Will I be able to sleep through military action?

You will get used to the noise. During the Gulf War, said one soldier, "the engineers began to blow up everything the Iraqi army had left behind. Every few minutes an explosion would send smoke clouds way into the air. At first I was startled by the force and concussion of each explosion. But, as time went on, I stopped noticing the blasts and even fell asleep to them. What amazed me was how the body became conditioned to the noise. Most sane people would be terrified after hearing one Iraqi ammunition dump explode. We no longer noticed."[42]

What happens if I am subjected to long periods without sleep?

Lack of sleep will severely impair your ability to function in combat. You lose about 25 percent of your mental ability after staying awake for 24 hours. The same is true if you only get 4 to 5 hours of sleep for five days or more. However, studies have shown that once you make up this sleep deficit, there is no lasting medical or psychological harm.[43]

How heavy will my pack be?

You will carry heavy loads, even in warm weather. The average cold-weather load is 101.5 pounds. The average warm-weather load is 88.3 pounds. Carrying a heavy pack into combat gives you more fighting options, but it slows you down and is tiring.[44]

Will I be able to breathe if I have to fight at high altitudes?

Headaches, lethargy, lack of appetite, exhaustion, dehydration, and weight loss are characteristic of operations at high altitude. High altitude increases energy requirements by as much as 50 percent. You will become accustomed to the thinner air, but you will lose weight. The average weight loss for one special forces team working with the Pakistan army's High-Altitude Mountain School in 1994 was 20 to 25 pounds. You must control weight loss before it becomes incapacitating. Weight loss leads to fatigue, loss of strength, and psychological change, such as decreased mental capacity and alertness, along with low morale. All of these conditions can contribute to accidents and a failure to accomplish your mission.[45]

What will I eat at high altitudes?

You will be fed a diet rich in carbohydrates. You should eat a variety of foods, and plan snacks. Drink four to six quarts of non-caffeinated beverages a day and monitor the color and volume of your urine for possible dehydration (dark yellow means take action). Do not skip meals, although you will not feel like eating. Consume a little of everything in your ration. Do not eat fatty foods or consume alcohol.[46]

What do enlisted men and women think about their officers?

Differences in rank and superior-subordinate relationships are the source of most conflict within the military. There can be animosity between lower-ranking enlisted personnel and officers or direct supervisors. This arises from the intense closeness of the working situation, the fact that officers are responsible for overseeing the unpleasant "housekeeping" details, and the virtual absence of officers from the barracks unless they are conducting inspections.[47]

What are my chances of being wounded or killed if we go to war?

About 1 in 5, if you fight with the infantry in a major war. If you are in a non-infantry position, the odds of being wounded or killed fall to about 1 in 50. The overall odds for becoming a casualty if you are deployed to a war zone in a military capacity are about 1 in 15. In World War II, 6.6 percent of all Americans serving were wounded or killed. 7.8 percent of all U.S. servicemen deployed to the Korean War were wounded or killed, as were 6.2 of all military personnel deployed to the Vietnam War. Shorter wars are much safer. Only .13 percent of the forces deployed to the Gulf War were wounded or killed. However, psychiatric casualty rates remain high. Up to 30 percent of Vietnam veterans had lasting psychological consequences of their time in battle, as did up to 20 percent of Gulf War veterans.[48]

Chapter 4

WEAPONS AND WOUNDS

What will a bullet do to my body?

It will damage or destroy tissue. A bullet must travel at 80 meters per second to penetrate your skin. When a bullet leaves an AK-47 it is traveling at 980 meters per second (730 meters per second when fired from an M-16). The shape of the bullet, how it is moving toward you, and where it enters determine how much damage you will sustain. Bullets that fragment on impact, bullets that "tumble" after penetrating your skin, and bullets that strike you at an oblique angle will do more damage than bullets that hit you directly and travel straight through your body while remaining in one piece.[1]

What are the best and worst places to get shot?

A clean line through your arm, hand, or foot is best, though it will be painful. Bullets damage in different ways depending on where they hit. The pressure from a bullet that enters the brain will usually rupture the skull. Low-density tissue like lungs offer less resistance, but a lung wound will make it very difficult to breathe. The spleen, liver, and kidney may rupture on impact. The damage to your stomach depends on what you have in it. An empty stomach is better. If you have water or food in your stomach, the bullet will push it outward against your organs. Nerve damage from a bullet can result in loss of feeling and temporary paralysis. Bullets often sever blood vessels rather than rupture them. If you are hit in an artery you will bleed to death very quickly unless you receive medical attention.[2]

What does it feel like to be shot?

Here is George Orwell's account of being shot by a sniper in the Spanish Civil War:

> Roughly speaking it was the sensation of being at the centre of an explosion. There seemed to be a loud bang and a blinding flash of light all round me, and I felt a tremendous shock—no pain, only a violent shock, such as you get from an electric terminal; with it a sense of utter weakness, a feeling of being stricken and shriveled up to nothing. I fancy you would feel much the same if you were struck by lightning. I knew immediately that I was hit, but because of the seeming bang and flash I thought it was a rifle nearby that had gone off accidentally and shot me. All this happened in a space of time much less than a second. The next moment my knees crumpled up and I was falling, my head hitting the ground with a violent bang which, to my relief, did not hurt. I had a numb, dazed feeling, a consciousness of being very badly hurt, but no pain in the ordinary sense.[3]

What part of my body is most likely to be wounded?

Your legs. In a war fought with conventional weapons, the legs and feet account for approximately 40 percent of all injuries. Arms and hands account for 25 percent of injuries. Head and neck injuries account for 15 percent, and chest injuries account for 10 percent. Abdomen and pelvis injuries account for the last 10 percent.[4]

In what part of my body is a wound most likely to be fatal?

The head. Head and neck wounds account for roughly 40 percent of combat deaths.[5]

If I am wounded, what are the odds I will die?

About one in five. Fragmentation mortar bombs and grenades kill about 10 percent of those they wound. Conventional artillery shells kill about 20 percent of those they wound. If you are shot, there is a one in three chance you will die.[6]

If I am wounded when my vehicle is hit by fire, what are the odds I will die?

Much higher. Antitank and antiaircraft weapons kill between 40 and 80 percent of all the troops they injure.[7]

What type of injury should I be most afraid of?

In general, bullet injuries are more lethal, but fragmentation injuries are more common.[8]

Are these injuries as common in the Navy and Air Force?

No. Because of their distance from ground combat, and the time they spend in confined spaces, the greatest threat to sailors and airmen is burns.[9]

Can a bullet get through body armor?

The bullet should stop before it penetrates your skin. If it does go through your vest, it will be slowed down, losing much of its wounding power. Body armor is most effective against small fragments and low-velocity bullets. High-velocity bullets, such as AK-47 rounds, can penetrate parts of your body armor, such as your back and flank where there is less protection. It is probably best to take a bullet in the chest. You may be left with bruises or broken bones, but the plate in your armor should stop the bullet.[10]

Can I die if I am shot in the arm or leg?

Yes. A high-velocity bullet will create ripples in your bloodstream throughout your body, like a stone thrown into a pool of water, and cause widespread damage. A thigh wound from a fragmenting bullet can sever arteries, causing you to bleed to death.[11]

How dangerous are ricochet bullets?

A ricochet bullet—a bullet or fragment of a bullet that has hit another surface before hitting your body—can cause more damage than a normal bullet. The initial impact will absorb some of the bullet's energy, but it will also deform the round and cause it to tumble. The result will be a bullet or fragment coming at you at a lower velocity, but with a greater potential to cause wounds. These types of projectiles can cause large entrance wounds and more widespread damage to your internal tissue. However, some ricochets will be slowed down or reduced to the point where the damage they cause is superficial.[12]

At what distance am I safe from a sniper?

The longest confirmed kill on record is 2,500 yards, well over a mile. The shooter was an American soldier in Vietnam. Sniper bullets are effective at more than one kilometer.[13]

Will my helmet protect me from a head wound?

Yes. Your helmet can either deflect or slow a bullet significantly. During the Gulf War, the hospitals attached to the U.S. Army Seventh Corps found that the only soldiers with head wounds who sustained a brain injury were wounded in the forehead, which their helmets did not cover. In the Battle of Mogadishu in 1993, 5 of the 18 combat deaths resulted from head wounds. The four bullets that caused fatal brain injuries in these deaths entered in areas not protected by the helmet. Little is known about the exact effect of taking a bullet or fragment to the helmet. In one case, a bullet penetrated the helmet of a Ranger in Somalia, striking him on the back of his skull and causing a minor laceration, brain contusion, and momentary blindness.[14]

Should men try to protect their genitals in combat?

There is not much you can do. Your groin is not protected by body armor. However, genital wounds accounted for only about 1 percent of the injuries among the military in Somalia, and penis wounds alone account for a small minority of genital injuries. Most wounds are to the scrotum.[15]

What do artillery shells do to you?

Artillery shells can wound or kill you in several ways. Most shells are designed to detonate on impact, a few feet above the target, or with a time delay. The extent of your injuries often depends on how close you are to the blast. A combination of heat, the blast effect, and shrapnel will kill you if you are directly hit. The heat and blast pressure will dissipate the farther from the explosion, but shrapnel from a small shell will spray out 200 feet in all directions. Shrapnel fragments from a large shell can travel almost half a mile. Shrapnel causes injuries similar to fragmented bullets. These fragments wobble along their flight path and can strike your body at a high velocity—in some cases, at almost twice the velocity of an AK-47 round (1,798 meters per second). The shrapnel can fragment even further inside your body.[16]

How much force does an explosion create?

The detonation of high explosives creates a pressure wave moving at 3,000 meters per second (more than 6,000 miles per hour). The force of the blow is similar to being hit by a truck. In an enclosed space, where the blast is contained, even a hand grenade can cause severe internal damage.[17]

If I can walk away from an explosion, does it mean I am OK?

No. Even if an explosion does not kill you with heat or shrapnel, the pressure wave itself may damage your body. These are "silent injuries." You may be free of symptoms for up to 48 hours after the blast. The pressure can enter your lungs and rupture air sacs. It can cause severe respiratory distress that can be fatal. You can be injured due to the "spalling effect" of a pressure wave. This is the same effect that causes rusty flakes on the inside of a pipe to come off when it is struck by a hammer. Your organs may be ruptured even if your skin is not broken. Your eardrum may also be ruptured, causing deafness. Without infection, a ruptured eardrum will heal. A ruptured eardrum may indicate internal injuries.[18]

What kinds of mines will I encounter?

There are two major types of land mines: blast mines, which usually explode from pressure, and fragmentation mines, which are usually triggered by wires or remote control. Blast mines can be targeted to personnel or vehicles (hence, "anti-tank mines"). Fragmentation mines are designed solely to inflict human casualties.[19]

What will happen if I step on a land mine?

Anti-personnel land mines carry 30 to 300 grams of high explosives. A 30-gram mine will blow your foot off, or damage your foot to the extent that it will have to be amputated. One in three cases will have head or eye injuries from penetrating fragments. A 150-gram mine will shred your legs to midthigh. Anti-personnel mines are designed to severely injure, not kill, because of the increased burden caring for injured personnel puts on a unit.[20]

What if my armored vehicle triggers an anti-tank mine?

Your vehicle's armor will protect you from the fragments generated from the explosion. You will be injured by the blast wave. The injuries will include those you would see in a car accident: hearing loss, a broken back and severed spinal cord, and damage to your lungs, heart, and brain. Any organ in your body that has air in it will be susceptible to damage.[21]

What if I trigger a fragmentation mine?

Unlike blast mines, which are typically hidden or buried on the ground, fragmentation mines explode at a height of one to two meters. This is accomplished either by placing the mines on rods at that height or by using mines that jump up from ground level before exploding. They are often interconnected in a series of three to six mines to concentrate the killing power. Explosion velocity is close to 1,000 meters per second. If you are not killed by the blast wave you may be killed or injured by the needle fragments of the explosion, which can be lethal to soldiers up to 50 meters away.[22]

What will happen to me if I am wounded by a hand grenade?

Modern hand grenades can be lethal in a radius of up to 150 feet. A thousand fragments can explode from a single hand grenade at 2,000 meters per second. Some grenade fragments are made from glass fiber and do not appear on an X ray.[23]

What kinds of aircraft bombs will be used against me?

There are two types of bombs: fragmentation and blast bombs. Some fragmentation bombs can penetrate armored steel from 50 yards away. Blast bombs include fuel-air mixtures with multiple detonations. The first detonation, 5 to 10 meters above the ground, disperses a concentrated fuel mixture. The second detonation, a fraction of a second later, ignites the fuel while it is in the air. This creates a massive, deadly fireball.[24]

What happens if I am hit by an explosive that does not detonate?

The surgeon will determine your probability of survival. You will be taken away from the operating area if the surgeon does not expect you to survive. There, an explosive ordnance technician will defuse the weapon. If the surgeon thinks you can survive, and the round will not detonate, it will be removed.[25]

What is an incendiary weapon?

A weapon that uses flame or heat on its targets. Such weapons include napalm (thickened oil), depleted uranium, magnesium, thermite, and phosphorous used in warheads and ammunition. Napalm was banned by a U.N. agreement in 1980.[26]

What kind of injuries do incendiaries cause?

Severe burns. Magnesium and thermite burns are small but deep. Phosphorous can burn for hours, and has toxic effects on the liver, kidneys, and heart. Napalm typically burns much of the body. It burns for a long time, creates toxic vapors, and often suffocates its victims.[27]

What happens if I am burned?

You can go into shock. Burns have serious internal effects. Severe burns can cause extreme loss of fluid, organ failure, circulatory system failure, immune system dysfunction, fever, infection, and vomiting, as well as breathing problems due to inhalation of chemicals and heat. Burns also damage your blood's ability to clot, making blood loss a critical problem.[28]

How should I be treated if burned?

Your wound must be cooled and cleaned. Your bleeding must be stopped. You might need an immediate blood transfusion and breathing help, including oxygen and assisted ventilation. You will need extra nutrition and fluid. You might receive early skin grafts. If you have a chemical burn, the chemical must be removed before treatment, usually with water. If water is poured on phosphorous, however, it boils and spreads, causing more damage.[29]

What are the long-term effects of burns?

If you live, you may be incapacitated for life. You may have severe scarring, and require skin grafts or reconstructive surgery. Your resistance to disease may be lowered, and you may have chronic pain. You may also have to face the social stigma of burn scars.[30]

Will I be exposed to radioactive munitions?

Probably, but in very low levels. Depleted uranium, a byproduct of the production of enriched uranium (used in nuclear power generation and nuclear warheads), is two and a half times as hard as steel. The U.S. military uses depleted uranium in some armor-piercing shells and bullets, and in tank armor. Depleted uranium munitions can be fired as 120-millimeter rounds from an M-1 tank or 30-millimeter rounds from an A-10 Thunderbolt. If depleted uranium enters your system, it can cause permanent damage to your kidneys, or lesions on your bones and liver. In the Gulf War, soldiers in vehicles hit by friendly fire were exposed to depleted uranium through inhalation, ingestion, and contamination of open wounds. Others might have been exposed to battle dust and contaminated smoke. The long-term health effects are not known.[31]

How can I avoid depleted uranium contamination?

Depleted uranium particles will linger in the area where a munition exploded. If you are asked to clean up a destroyed tank or remove munitions, wear your chemical suit.[32]

What if I am in a helicopter crash?

You may break your back and sever your spinal cord. There is a chance you will break your legs. Nonfatal spinal injuries can result in varying degrees of paralysis.[33]

How am I most likely to be wounded or killed?

Artillery shells cause most wounds. About 65 percent (340,000) of those wounded in World War II were hit by shells. Small arms caused about 25 percent of that war's wounds, and land mines, about 5 percent. In the Israel-Lebanon war, artillery and mortars caused about 25 percent of the wounded and dead, followed by small arms (20 percent) and rocket-propelled grenades (15 percent). In Vietnam, 42 percent of casualties on search-and-destroy missions were from bullets, and 50 percent were from fragmentation (mines, bombs, and grenades). For those injured or killed in Vietnam while assigned to base defense, 80 percent of casualties were from fragmentation, and only 16 percent were from bullets.[34]

What are the consequences of losing too much blood?

If you lose more than two liters of blood, you will go into circulatory shock. Your heart will beat rapidly, up to twice per second. Without the oxygen that the blood delivers, vital organs may be permanently damaged. After an hour, your liver will start to pump waste into your blood. You will go into cardiac depression and may suffer a heart attack and brain damage.[35]

How can I tell how much blood I have lost?

Do not rely on your visual assessment. A wound yielding 100 milliliters (100 cubic centimeters) of blood can cause a stain on cloth up to 15 inches wide. You need to lose 10 times as much blood as this to be at risk.[36]

Will a medic attend to me right away?

Probably not. Military medical triage is very sophisticated, and in only 10 to 20 percent of injuries is immediate care the difference between life and death. If the medics can wait to pay attention to you, they will, to keep themselves free for those who require immediate care. Between 60 and 80 percent of injuries will not require a doctor's attention on the battle-field. You may be stabilized by a combat lifesaver (Army) or Navy Corpsman (Navy and Marines) and evacuated. Ten percent of injuries will be too severe to warrant any treatment.[37]

If a medic has to operate on me in the field, will he or she have anesthesia?

Probably, but he or she may not use it. Anesthetics can have side effects, such as causing you to vomit or masking symptoms that could aid in the diagnosis of your injury. If the medic does not have time to fully assess your injury, he or she may proceed without anesthesia.[38]

If I have to get to a hospital, will I make it in time?

Probably. The U.S. military is supported by a sophisticated medical evacuation system. It will use the first available plane to move you, within two hours if necessary. The current medevac system is a consequence of a recent shift in national military strategy that includes an "evacuate and replace" philosophy to keep battlefield forces fresh. This philosophy has successfully reduced casualty rates for U.S. forces.[39]

If I make it to the hospital, will I survive?

Not always. War wounds are dirty. Infection sets in within four to six hours. This can be countered with drugs, but even the newest antibiotics and surgical techniques have not reduced the rate of postoperative infections. Infections account for 10 to 20 percent of hospital deaths in war.[40]

What will happen to me psychologically if I am badly wounded?

Initially, you will be in shock. In this state you will be unable to understand information given to you. You may exhibit indifference and depression. For one to two weeks after the injury, you will be aggressive and anxious. After one to three weeks you will begin accommodating yourself to your new situation. You will be able to work with your doctor on a plan for your long-term mental and physical rehabilitation.[41]

What is the most common mistake in war surgery?

Missed multiple injuries in the same patient. Once your medic identifies your first injury he or she should start looking for your second, and third. What the medic thinks is your exit wound may really be the entry wound for a second bullet.[42]

If I survive my injury, what are the odds I will be discharged?

About one in five. Being injured by a land mine gives you the highest chance of being discharged, at 32 percent. Being hit by a bullet, if you survive, gives you a 30 percent chance of a permanent discharge. Being hit by fragments from a shell or grenade give you a 20 percent chance of discharge (one in five), and from a bomb 16 percent (one in six).[43]

How long will I be out of action if I am injured?

It depends what you were injured by. In World War II, if you were injured by a bomb, your average "days noneffective" were 94. In order of incapacitation, the next most harmful were a grenade (104 days), a shell (123 days), a bullet (158 days), and a land mine (174 days).[44]

What is the most painful way to be wounded?

Being burned. Burns can cover the entire body. It is difficult to dull the pain. Burns have historically accounted for 3 percent of combat injuries, though they are becoming more common as soldiers spend an increasing amount of time in tanks and armored vehicles. During the Yom Kippur War, 10 percent of all injured soldiers were burned. In the Falkland Islands conflict, 18 percent of all British casualties were burned. In the U.S. military, members of the Navy and Air Force are more likely to be burned than those in the Army.[45]

What is the basic U.S. rifle?

The M16A2, more commonly known as the M-16. The first version of this rifle, the M16A1, was created by Colt in the early 1960s, then modified and adopted by the U.S. military. The M16A2 replaced the M16A1 in the mid-1990s. It is a gas-operated, magazine-fed, shoulder- or hip-fired weapon designed for either automatic fire (three-round bursts) or semiautomatic fire (single shot). It costs approximately $600. The Army also uses the M-4, a shortened version of the M-16 which is easier to maneuver in jungle and urban combat.[46]

Q: What is the basic bullet?

The 5.56-millimeter M16A2 round, which begins to tumble when it strikes the skin to cause maximum tissue damage.[47]

What will the enemy use?

Probably the AK-47. More than 70 million AK-47s, or Kalashnikovs, have been produced since 1947. Almost 80 countries and countless guerrilla groups use the weapon. In comparison, eight million M-16s, the second-most-produced assault rifle, have been made.[48]

What kind of bullet will the enemy use?

Probably a 7.62-millimeter full mantle. The Yugoslavian-type hollow point 7.62 AK-47 round begins to tumble after impact, but is not as damaging as the M16A2 round.[49]

What is a dumdum bullet?

It is a bullet that is either scored or has a soft or hollow point. The name comes from a British military arsenal in Dum-Dum, India, where the original dumdum was developed by removing one millimeter of the bullet's jacket. These bullets were so devastating to human tissue they were outlawed in 1899 at the Hague Conference. The original M16A1 round was almost as devastating as the nineteenth-century dumdum in terms of its tendency to fragment. The new M16A2 bullets are even more damaging, fragmenting earlier to cause more damage as soon as they hit the skin.[50]

What does a dumdum bullet do to you?

A dumdum bullet is more likely to fragment or "mushroom" either in flight or after entering your body. The wounds these bullets cause range from ruptured organs to bones splintered into particles. The exit wound from a 5.56-millimeter bullet in the thigh can be up to four inches in diameter.[51]

What is the biggest gun I will use on individual enemy fighters?

That may depend on your commander. One soldier recalled, "In basic training we were told that it was illegal to use a 50-caliber machine gun against soldiers, but that it could be used to target enemy equipment. Accordingly, to circumvent this legal restriction, the drill sergeants suggested we aim at the equipment worn by the enemy soldiers, rather than at the soldiers themselves."[52]

What is a cluster bomb?

A cluster bomb can deliver from three to more than a thousand fragmentation bombs through a single mechanism. The carrier missile is launched by cannon or mortar, or as a rocket or an airplane bomb. While still in the air, the carrier releases its payload of bombs, which then separate and explode. A single cluster bomb can cover 50,000 square meters (more than two football fields square) with antipersonnel fragments. Cluster weapons provide saturation fire across a wide ground area. They are the tactical equivalent of short-range nuclear weapons.[53]

What is the enemy's most effective weapon against me?

A gun. Any soldier hit by a bullet is likely to be taken out of action. One third of such soldiers die, and another third are removed from the battlefield (with many of those being permanently discharged). Only one third of soldiers hit by a bullet return to combat quickly.[54]

Chapter 5

WEAPONS OF MASS DESTRUCTION

What are weapons of mass destruction?

Weapons of mass destruction, typically abbreviated WMD, include all nuclear, biological, and chemical munitions. They are also sometimes grouped together under the heading "NBC," for nuclear, biological, and chemical.[1]

What are nuclear weapons and why are they so powerful?

There are two types of nuclear bombs: fission and fusion. Fission bombs derive their force from the energy that is produced by splitting atoms. Fusion bombs—the more powerful of the two—get their energy by fusing atoms together. The energy created by the atomic process is released at tremendous speed (in about one millionth of a second).[2]

How are nuclear bombs delivered?

Nuclear weapons can be delivered by aerial bombardment, short- and medium-range ballistic missiles, rockets, aircraft, and field artillery.[3]

What happens during a nuclear attack?

A nuclear attack has four main characteristics. First there is a blast, which produces an intense shock wave and high-power winds capable of collapsing shelters. The second is thermal radiation, which produces intense heat and light that causes burns and starts fires. The third is nuclear radiation, which has two phases: initial and residual. Initial radiation comes directly from the fireball in the first minute after the bomb has gone off. Residual radiation lingers after the first minute, and can be a hazard for years. Depending on weather conditions, radioactive fallout can spread for hundreds of miles. Fourth is a massive surge of electrical power created at the instant of detonation and transmitted at the speed of light in all directions. Its effects travel to the visual horizon as seen from the detonation point. If the device bursts at high altitude, it can cause electrical problems across an entire continent.[4]

What could happen to me in a nuclear attack?

If you are not killed immediately by the blast or thermal burns, exposure to nuclear radiation can kill you by destroying or damaging the cells of your body. This cell damage causes "radiation sickness," the severity of which depends on how much radiation you receive, how long you are exposed, and the condition of your body at the time. Initial symptoms of radiation sickness can include headache, nausea, vomiting, and diarrhea, and usually appear within one to six hours after exposure. The majority of people suffering from severe radiation sickness die within the first two weeks of exposure. For survivors, long-term consequences, including the development of various forms of cancer, are due mainly to radiation and psychological trauma.[5]

What will happen if I am exposed to nuclear radiation but do not die immediately?

The Office of the Surgeon General's *Textbook of Military Medicine* states:

> Fatally irradiated soldiers should receive every possible palliative treatment, including narcotics, to prolong their utility and alleviate their physical and psychological distress. Depending on the amount of fatal radiation, such soldiers may have several weeks to live and to devote to the cause. Commanders and medical personnel should be familiar with estimating survival time based on onset of vomiting. Physicians should be prepared to give medications to alleviate diarrhea, and to prevent infection and other sequelae of radiation sickness in order to allow the soldier to serve as long as possible. The soldier must be allowed to make the full contribution to the war effort. He will already have made the ultimate sacrifice. He deserves a chance to strike back, and to do so while experiencing as little discomfort as possible.[6]

How many people have died from nuclear weapons?

There have been two nuclear attacks. During World War II, bombs were dropped on Hiroshima and Nagasaki, Japan, on August 6 and 9, 1945. The bombs killed 64,000 in Hiroshima and 39,000 in Nagasaki. Thousands more died afterward from the short- and long-term effects of exposure.[7]

What should I do if we come under nuclear attack?

The best thing to do is take cover behind a hill or in a fighting position or ditch. If you are caught out in the open, drop to the ground, close your eyes, and cover all exposed skin as much as possible. If possible, lie with your head facing away from the blast, and do not look at it. It could blind you. Stay down until the blast wave passes and then check for injuries and equipment damage. Take potassium iodide pills to protect yourself against radioactive iodine, even three to four hours after detonation. The pills will not protect you against other radioactive substances.[8]

Is it likely that I will face a nuclear attack while at war?

It is doubtful. Nuclear weapons are seen as impractical in war because they contaminate the area of detonation for a very long time. Radioactive fallout can spread over a wide area, hitting the attacker's own troops and territory.[9]

What is a dirty bomb?

Dirty bombs are made by wrapping radioactive material around a conventional explosive (like TNT). Though they can not create nuclear explosions, dirty bombs can cause widespread dissemination of radioactive particles. Immediate evacuation would be necessary for tens of city blocks. Tens of miles around the blast center would be contaminated. In a dirty bomb explosion, some would die from the blast itself, as in any explosion. The radioactive fallout would spread over several city blocks. It would cause the same types of injuries and casualties as radioactive fallout from a nuclear weapon.[10]

Have dirty bombs been used before?

No, but they are considered a credible threat. In May 2002 an alleged terrorist was arrested in the U.S. for plotting to build and explode a dirty bomb. Iraq tested a one-ton dirty bomb in 1987, but abandoned the idea because the bomb would not generate radiation levels deadly enough to inflict significant casualties.[11]

Is it difficult to make a dirty bomb?

It is as easy as making conventional bombs. The hard part is acquiring and handling the radioactive material, which can cause injury or death.[12]

What are biological weapons?

Biological weapons include viruses, bacteria, other microorganisms, and toxins derived from living organisms that are used to injure or kill humans, animals, or plants. The U.S. has renounced biological warfare, but many other nations have not.[13]

What are some biological weapons?

Bacterial agents include anthrax, brucellosis, cholera, glanders, melioidosis, plague, Q fever, and tularemia. Viral agents include smallpox, Venezuelan equine encephalitis, and viral hemorrhagic fevers. Toxins include ricin, botulinum nerve toxin, and others.[14]

Which biological weapons am I most likely to encounter?

Smallpox, anthrax, and botulism are among the most likely threats. In theory, any infectious agent or toxic chemical could be engineered for use as a weapon.[15]

How are biological weapons delivered?

Biological weapons can be delivered with sprays (by generators) or as aerosolized spores (by explosives, bomblets, missiles, and aircraft). Food and water can also be contaminated, or infected flies, mosquitos, fleas, and ticks can be released.[16]

What are the long-term effects of biological weapons?

Long-term and delayed health effects of biological weapons include chronic illness, mutation, developmental irregularities, cancer, and effects caused by ecological change.[17]

Will I be able to tell if I am being exposed to biological weapons?

No. Aerosols of biological weapons agents and contamination of food or water supplies are not detectable by the human senses. The military uses detection systems, but they are limited. Before the Iraqi War, Marines in Kuwait used chickens as an early warning system for biological agents. The chickens were ineffective, often worrying themselves to death.[18]

What is anthrax?

Anthrax is a bacterial disease that is usually carried by mammals and birds. Three types of anthrax affect humans: cutaneous (which enters the skin through a cut or abrasion), gastrointestinal tract anthrax (contracted if you eat contaminated food), and inhalation anthrax (contracted by breathing in air borne anthrax spores). The cutaneous form accounts for 95 percent of naturally occurring human cases, but the inhalation form poses the greatest threat as a biological weapon. Anthrax is considered an ideal biological weapon because it is not contagious, so there is little chance of it infecting the attacking forces as well.[19]

What could anthrax do to me?

Inhalation anthrax has an incubation period of one to six days. After this, you may exhibit flu-like symptoms such as headaches, muscle pain, fever, and coughing. Later symptoms include high fever, breathing difficulties, skin discoloration, and shock.[20]

Will I die if I am exposed to anthrax?

It is possible. You can fully recover with antibiotic treatment if it is provided less than 48 hours after your symptoms appear. Untreated cutaneous anthrax is fatal in 5 to 20 percent of cases. Untreated inhalation anthrax is fatal in 80 percent of cases.[21]

What is smallpox?

Smallpox is a highly contagious and potentially fatal virus. The most common form of smallpox causes acute onset of fever, chills, headache, backache, vomiting, skin lesions, and sometimes delirium.[22]

How common is smallpox?

Smallpox was eradicated in 1979. Stockpiles of the virus exist in two maximum-security locations in the U.S. and Russia. The genomic sequence for smallpox is known, published, and can be duplicated. A single case of smallpox would be a global emergency.[23]

How could I get smallpox?

If used as a biological weapon, smallpox would probably be distributed through aerosolized spores. You could also catch it from someone who had been infected.[24]

Will I die if I am exposed to smallpox?

Between 20 and 40 percent of people infected with the most common form of smallpox die. Because smallpox is a virus, it does not respond to antibiotics the way anthrax does. But symptoms of the virus—fever, pain, secondary bacterial infections—can be treated. There are effective pre- and postexposure vaccinations, the latter of which can be administered up to four days after exposure. Vaccinations provide high immunity for three to five years.[25]

How many people have died from smallpox?

In the twentieth century, smallpox killed between 300 and 500 million people. It is one of the most devastating diseases known to humankind.[26]

What is botulism?

Botulism is a noncontagious but potentially fatal disease caused by exposure to botulinum nerve toxin, the most toxic substance known to science. If you are infected, you may experience dry mouth, bowel obstruction, constipation, and urinary retention within 12 to 36 hours. Later symptoms can include muscle paralysis, which can cause the upper respiratory system to fail.[27]

How do I get botulism?

The primary threat during war is delivery by airborne spores, though you can also become sick with botulism if you eat food contaminated with the botulinum toxin. A preexposure vaccine has been developed, though it is not clear if it is effective in humans. There is an immune serum that can stop the toxin from circulating in the body. This serum can prevent respiratory failure and death.[28]

Have biological weapons ever been used in war?

Yes. In the ancient world, Roman armies used the corpses of humans and animals to contaminate water. During the French and Indian War in the mid-1700s, the British gave blankets contaminated with scales from smallpox victims to American Indians, killing as much as 30 percent of some tribes. During World War II, Japanese planes reportedly dropped rice, wheat grains, cotton, and paper infected with plague bacillus over the Chinese village of Changteh, causing an estimated 700 deaths. The Japanese were also accused of using typhoid, cholera, and dysentery to poison more than 1,000 Manchurian wells. During the civil war in Rhodesia in the late 1970s, the Rhodesian military was suspected of air-dropping anthrax spores into guerrilla zones, which resulted in 10,000 human cases of anthrax and 182 deaths.[29]

Can biological weapons destroy my unit?

Not necessarily. Rapid-acting toxins may be effective, but most biological munitions are poor tactical weapons on the modern battlefield. They have incubation periods of several days to weeks, so the ramifications of a biological attack might not be realized until after the outcome of the battle is determined.[30]

What are chemical weapons?

Chemical weapons are like pesticides, only much more powerful. They are typically released over large areas. Chemicals known to have been developed into chemical warfare agents can be divided into two categories: lethal chemicals and disabling chemicals. The former group of chemicals is meant to kill, the latter group to take an enemy out of action for a temporary period of time.[31]

What are some chemical weapons?

There are two types of lethal chemicals: tissue irritants (choking gases and blister gases) and systemic poisons (blood and nerve gases). There are also two types of disabling chemicals: incapacitants and harassing agents (like tear gas).[32]

Which chemical weapons agents am I most likely to encounter on the battlefield?

Sarin and VX (nerve gases), mustard gas (blister gas), hydrogen cyanide (blood gas), CS or CN (tear gas), and phosgene (choking agent) are some of the chemical weapons agents that you may encounter. A mixture of these agents may be used to cause confusion and increase their killing power.[33]

Are chemical weapons easy to make?

Yes. It takes no more money or expertise to produce chemical weapons than it does to produce conventional munitions.

The technology and literature needed to produce chemical weapons are readily available. Stockpiles can be quickly amassed once an enemy has decided to make chemical weapons.[34]

How are chemical weapons delivered?

Chemical agents can be released as gases, liquids, or sprays, which can be delivered by artillery, mortars, rockets, missiles, aircraft, bombs, and land mines. Chemical agents are typically delivered via inhalation, ingestion, or absorption. Injection is also possible, but less likely.[35]

What is sarin?

Sarin, a nerve gas, acts by disrupting the normal functioning of the nervous system. Nerve agents in high enough doses have multiple effects: asphyxiation, sweating, drooling, vomiting, dimming of vision, heart failure, and epileptic seizures. These agents can kill within minutes. Nerve gas is normally disseminated through aerosol or vapor.[36]

What is mustard gas?

Mustard and other blister gases act by producing chemical burns. They affect the skin and respiratory tract. These agents can cause a powerful irritation of the eyes, nose, and skin. There is sometimes little or no pain upon exposure. Symptoms may be delayed for several hours or days. Severe exposure, particularly by inhalation, can kill you by preventing oxygen from reaching the tissues of the body. Mustard gas is normally disseminated through liquid or droplets.[37]

What does cyanide (blood gas) do and how does it work?

Cyanide acts by preventing oxygen from reaching cells. Symptoms include rapid breathing, convulsions, and coma. If you inhale high concentrations, it will kill you quickly. Cyanide is normally disseminated through aerosol or vapor.[38]

How do I protect myself against blood, blister, and nerve agents?

You should wear a protective mask and clothing.[39]

What do choking agents do and how do they work?

Choking agents, used in World War I, are the oldest type of chemical weapons. When delivered in sufficient concentrations, they cause the lungs to fill with fluid. This can cause you to choke to death. Choking agents are the least effective chemical weapons because they dissipate quickly.[40]

What does tear gas do and how does it work?

Tear gas is not deadly, except in extremely high concentrations. It is usually used in riot control. It can disable you by causing severe irritation of the eyes and respiratory tract. Symptoms are immediate upon exposure and usually disappear shortly after exposure. You will be exposed to tear gas in basic training to make sure your mask fits and works properly, and to help you avoid panic if you are exposed to it in combat.[41]

What can be done for me if the enemy attacks with incapacitating chemicals?

There is no special first aid to relieve the symptoms of incapacitating agents. You let the symptoms pass.[42]

What happens if I survive an attack by lethal chemical weapons?

You should be decontaminated immediately. This will minimize casualties and limit the spread of the agent. Decontamination usually involves using a water-based caustic or bleach material to neutralize chemical agents.[43]

If I survive a chemical attack, will I suffer consequences later in life?

The long-term effects of these weapons have not been studied as thoroughly as the immediate effects, but they may include chronic physical and mental illness. Iranian victims of Iraq's use of mustard gas in the 1980s experienced debilitating long-term diseases of the lungs, eyes, and skin. After World War I, people exposed to mustard gas reported widespread chronic debilitating lung disease.[44]

How do I know if I am being exposed to chemical weapons agents?

You may not be able to detect the presence of chemical agents. Most are odorless, colorless, tasteless, and invisible. Your unit should have chemical agent alarms and detection kits.[45]

Have chemical weapons been used before?

Yes. Since the end of World War II, chemical weapons have been used in Yemen (1960s), Laos and Cambodia (late 1970s), and Afghanistan (mid-1980s). In 1988, following the Iran-Iraq War, Saddam Hussein employed chemical weapons against the Kurds in Iraq, which killed thousands. A sarin attack by a Japanese cult in the Tokyo subway system in 1995 caused 11 deaths and more than 5,000 emergency medical evaluations.[46]

How effective are chemical weapons?

Chemical weapons are very unreliable and unpredictable. Their effectiveness relies on favorable weather conditions. They cannot be used to disable entire armies or cities. They are less destructive than other weapons. Protection and defensive measures greatly reduce the impact on the battlefield against well-trained troops.[47]

What should I do in the event of a chemical or biological attack?

Stop breathing. Put on your mask. Clear and check it. Give the alarm determined by your unit. If you develop symptoms of nerve agent poisoning, inject yourself with a nerve agent antidote from your nerve agent antidote kit.[48]

Will protective gear save me from nuclear, biological, or chemical exposure?

It can if it is worn properly. Protection gear will distort your visual, auditory, and tactile perceptions. Your motor coordination will be impaired, you will need to exert more physical effort. You will be more fatigued. Protective gear retains body heat. It increases the risk of heat exhaustion and heat stroke. It will be hard to recognize comrades and gauge their mood. Your unit may fall apart. You may feel helpless and isolated. This is a prime factor in battle fatigue. Claustrophobic panic, premature unmasking (which may be imitated by others), disorientation, and paranoid reactions to impaired sensory functioning may also occur. Training lessens some of these reflexes. These reactions are exacerbated when visibility is further restricted by darkness, smoke, or vegetation. Gas mask phobia proved to be a significant problem in the Allied invasion of Iraq during the Gulf War. Field studies have shown an increase in friendly fire casualties by insufficiently trained troops in protective gear. Whereas only about 1 in 20 soldiers or vehicles is shot by their own side in conventional battles, the rate rises as high as 1 in 5 in full protective gear. This is attributable to the combination of impaired vision and hearing, plus jumpiness.[49]

What are the psychological challenges of coming under chemical, biological, or nuclear attack?

They are unique and severe. According to a U.S. Army field manual,

The increased rate of destruction of potential future weaponry has both physical and psychological effects. Losing 40 to 60 percent of an entire unit in minutes or hours could leave the remaining soldiers incapacitated. The rapid and horrible death of comrades and leaders could have a definite and detrimental effect on the mental stability of the unit. Surviving soldiers will have to be prepared to overcome the experience of mass human destruction.[50]

Will I face biological and chemical weapons?

International treaties to which most countries have subscribed—the 1925 Geneva Protocol, the 1972 Biological and Toxin Weapons Convention, and the 1993 Chemical Weapons Convention—prohibit the development, production, and use of biological and chemical weapons. However, some countries have not signed these treaties. There are concerns that some of these countries, as well as terrorist groups, may use these weapons. The first choice would probably be chemicals.[51]

Are any countries known to have chemical or biological weapons programs?

Yes, and others have the capability to develop them quickly.

- North Korea has a chemical weapons program and developing biological weapons program.
- China has a chemical weapons program and an advanced biotechnology infrastructure.
- India has biological weapon and chemical weapon program capabilities.
- Pakistan has biological weapon and chemical weapon program capabilities.

- •Iran has biological weapon program capabilities and had a chemical weapon program (which it says it has eliminated).

- •Iraq, before the Gulf War, had the largest and most advanced biological warfare program in the Middle East.

- •Syria has biological and chemical weapon program capabilities.

- •Libya has a biological weapons program and chemical weapon capabilities.

- •Russia has biological and chemical weapons programs.

The United States actively researches lethal chemical and biological weapons but claims not to have stocks of them.[52]

Chapter 6

THE MOMENT OF COMBAT

How will my body react to combat?

Your brain will activate its "fight or flight" system. It will release a massive discharge of stress hormones. Your heart rate will jump from roughly 70 beats per minute to more than 200 beats per minute in less than a second. Blood flow to your large muscle masses will increase, making you stronger and faster. Minor blood vessels in your hands and feet will constrict, to reduce bleeding from wounds. Some common by-products of this reaction are tunnel vision, the loss of fine and complex motor control, and the inability to think clearly. If you are confronted with sudden danger you may not know how to react. You may not be able to see, think, or control your body. During the first experience of combat you may have a shaking fit or curl up in a fetal position. You will probably recover within a few days.[1]

How will I perform during my first time in combat?

Your performance may be poor. It will be hard for you to adjust, identify, and respond to dangers such as incoming artillery. You have a relatively high risk of being wounded or killed in your first battle.[2]

Will I get better?

Almost definitely. Once you get over your initial nervousness your combat skills will improve. You will learn to evaluate threats and quickly react to hostile movements and sounds. Over time you will learn to face battle calmly. If your unit suffers heavy casualties, or the chance of surviving a long war seems poor, your skills may decline.[3]

Will I fire my weapon?

Probably, although this was not always the case. Less than half the riflemen in World War II and 55 percent in the Korean War fired their weapons. U.S. military training has become more adept at conditioning you to shoot. Ninety percent of front-line personnel fired their weapons in Vietnam.[4]

What will make me fire?

You will fire based on commands from your leader, enemy contact, or the sudden appearance of a target. The farther you are from the enemy the easier it will be to pull the trigger. At close range, or in hand-to-hand combat, you will see the enemy as another human being and it will be harder to kill.[5]

Will it feel like training?

In some ways. In addition to fire and defense skills, you will receive stress inoculation training. The military attempts to replicate the noise, light, and intensity of combat. With enough training, war may feel like another exercise. As one Ranger recalled about Somalia, "I just started picking them out as they were running across the intersection two blocks away, and it was weird because it was so much easier than you would think. It was so much like basic training, they were just targets out there, and I don't know if it was the training that we had ingrained in us, but it seemed to me it was just like a moving target range and you could just hit the target and watch it all and it wasn't real."[6]

Will it feel like a video game?

It might. Since the 1980s the military has used video games for training. Games such as Doom, Battlezone, and Microsoft Flight Simulator have been adapted to introduce soldiers and Marines to combat. The Marines are developing at least one military tool with a six-button controller based on the console for the Sony PlayStation because many recruits are very familiar with the device.[7]

How can I avoid being shot by the enemy?

Avoid being seen. Rely on camouflage, physical defenses, and the cover of darkness. Stay low to the ground. Try not to stay up longer than three to five seconds so the enemy cannot track you. Minimize movement. Put tape around your dog tags so they do not make noise. Avoid wearing jewelry or using tape that can reflect sunlight. Use greasepaint to cover skin oils. Exposed skin, even dark skin, reflects light.[8]

How should I prepare for battle?

Get some sleep, eat, clean your weapon, and review your mission. The most motivated personnel are the most likely to ignore their need for food, water, and rest.[9]

Will I get used to combat?

Maybe. Some combat veterans develop a high tolerance for battlefield stress and fight calmly. You may experience anxiety afterward, however, as you look back at the fight and review close calls.[10]

What does it feel like to kill someone?

You will probably go through several emotional reactions when you kill. These are generally sequential, but not necessarily universal. The first phase is concern that you'll freeze up and won't be able to pull the trigger. The second is the actual kill, which, because of your training, will happen reflexively. You may feel exhilarated. Killing produces adrenaline; repeated killing can lead to a "killing addiction." This feeling can be especially intense if you kill at medium to long-range distances. The next phase, remorse and revulsion, can render you unable to ever kill again. Dave Grossman presents this "collage of pain and horror": ". . . my experience was one of revulsion and disgust . . . I dropped my weapon and cried . . . there was so much blood . . . I vomited . . . and I cried . . . I felt remorse and shame . . . I can remember whispering foolishly, 'I'm sorry' and then just throwing up." Only a few people are able to kill and not feel remorse, though many try to deny this feeling to make it easier to continue to kill. Subsequent killings are often easier to handle. Last is the rationalization and acceptance phase. This is a lifelong process during which you will try to account for what you did. Most are able to see what they did as the right and necessary thing. If you cannot rationalize your killing it may lead to post-traumatic stress disorder.[11]

Will I feel guilty killing in combat?

Most likely. After the exhilaration of killing, you will probably experience a feeling of remorse. This may be accompanied by thoughts that you are "sick" or "wrong" for having enjoyed killing. You may also have a profound feeling of responsibility for the dead—both comrades and enemies. Trying to reconcile this feeling of accountability will add more guilt. You may become agitated, angry or withdrawn. In the Gulf War, stress and guilt from killing enemy soldiers was reduced somewhat because much of the killing was done from long distances. Using group-fired weapons allows individuals to feel less responsible for enemy deaths. Military training seeks to depersonalize the enemy, making it easier for you to kill without guilt. Veteran officer J. Glenn Gray wrote: "Professional officers consider part of the psychological training of their troops to be training in hatred, and this becomes more systematized and subtler as the war goes on."[12]

Will I feel worse if I kill an enemy in an ambush?

You may. Those who kill in an ambush often find the experience disturbing. Many say it is hard to watch someone die. It is also hard to look at documents, letters, and photographs of loved ones on the bodies of someone you have killed.[13]

Is it easier to bear killing an enemy you cannot see?

Yes. The most traumatic reactions come from attacking someone you can clearly identify as a human being.[14]

Is there a chance I will enjoy killing?

Yes. Some people enjoy killing. Even those who do not can find it exciting. Vietnam veteran R. B. Anderson discussed the thrill of killing in combat in his essay "Vietnam Was Fun (?)": "It was fun . . . it was great fun. In combat I was a respected man among men. I lived on life's edge and did the most manly thing in the world: I was a warrior in war . . . Only a veteran can know about the thrill of the kill." Some people get stuck in the exhilaration phase of killing, which means that they are able to kill over and over without remorse. This can be especially true for snipers and pilots, whose killing is made easier by greater distance. Only about 2 percent of the population (3 to 4 percent of men and 1 percent of women) are considered "natural killers." This 2 percent typically accounts for up to 50 percent of the killing by a unit. The other 98 percent must overcome a natural resistance to killing. The intoxication of battle, however, can make killing attractive, even to those who do not at first find killing pleasant. J. Glenn Gray wrote: "Most men would never admit that they enjoy killing, and there are a great many who do not. On the other hand, thousands of youth who never suspected the presence of such an impulse in themselves have learned in military life the mad excitement of destroying."[15]

Will I have to kill an enemy with my bare hands?

Probably not, though you will be trained to do so.[16]

What will it be like to see dead bodies?

You may be struck by how similar the combatants are to you in age and appearance. You may be disgusted by the appearance and smell of the decaying flesh.[17]

How will I react to the enemy dead?

You may be full of rage and want to exact revenge from the corpses by violating the bodies. The impulse can be strong. Collecting scalps, ears, gold teeth, and other body parts as trophies is common when there is a strong hatred toward an enemy. Leaving deliberately mutilated bodies (especially with facial and genital mutilation) for the enemy to find is less common, but also occurs. You may also take pictures of yourself and your comrades next to the enemy's dead bodies.[18]

Will I be afraid?

Yes. Fear affects everyone in combat. You may fear dying. You may fear being afraid in front of your comrades. You may fear unknown weapons. You may fear causing grief to your family if you die.[19]

What will happen to my body if I am afraid?

In one division that saw heavy fighting in World War II, a quarter of the soldiers said they had been so scared during battle they vomited. A similar number said they had urinated or defecated in their pants in combat. This is a physical reaction to fear. It has nothing to do with your ability or willingness to fight.[20]

What happens to my mind if I am afraid?

It becomes harder to kill. When people are afraid or angry they do not think with their forebrain. They think with the midbrain. The midbrain harbors a deep instinct against killing one's own kind. The military combats this with repeated training. You will be rewarded for being able to overcome this instinct. It is the same principle used to train dogs.[21]

What are the negative aspects of my training?

The conflict between forebrain and midbrain may be the source of several long-term psychological consequences of combat and killing. Those who survive combat have a greater chance of depression and post traumatic stress disorder.[22]

What if I panic?

Panic can be deadly. You can become paralyzed. If you panic you may stand up under fire and try to run away. Panic puts you and others at risk. If you panic, those around you will probably try to restrain you.[23]

Will my unit forgive me if I panic?

Probably, if nobody was hurt. Panic is a common reaction. Your comrades want to know they can rely on you. If you get through the next battle without panic, they will probably assume you are reliable.[24]

Are all combat reactions negative?

No. Stress can make you more alert and responsive. The fight or flight response enlarges the pupils of your eyes, broadening your field of vision. You will be able to focus and react more quickly. At night, you may wake up during a mortar attack and take cover quickly before being hit. In battle you will be less apt to be distracted.[25]

Will I be willing to risk my life in combat?

Probably. You will want to protect the lives of your comrades. The biggest fear during battle is often not personal injury, but rather injury to comrades or letting comrades down. Bravery is not always a conscious decision. People who have carried out brave acts later refer to their heroism as "like watching myself in a movie" or an "out-of-body experience." J. Glenn Gray, who argues that friendship is not the same as comradeship, writes: "when a man dies for his friend, he does it deliberately and not in an ecstasy of emotion. Dying for one's comrades, on the other hand, is a phenomenon occurring in every war and can hardly be thought of as an act of superhuman courage. The impulse to self-sacrifice is an intrinsic element in the association of organized men in pursuit of a dangerous and difficult goal."[26]

Will I be decorated for bravery?

Probably not. Decorations are hard to earn. In World War II only one in four soldiers was decorated for bravery. Only 1.8 million decorations were awarded across a military force that was as large as 8.3 million men in May 1945.[27]

What are the highest decorations?

The Medal of Honor is the highest award for heroism. The second-highest ones are the Distinguished Service Cross (Army and Air Force) and Navy Cross (Navy and Marines), followed by the Silver Star Medal, which is awarded to all services.[28]

How common are those awards?

Less than 3,500 Medals of Honor have been awarded. In World War II, the Army awarded roughly 300 Medals of Honor, 4,500 Distinguished Service Crosses, and 75,000 Silver Stars— only 5 percent of all decorations given. In Vietnam, the Army awarded 155 Medals of Honor, 846 Distinguished Service Crosses, and 21,630 Silver Star Medals. The Marine Corps, which had 102,000 men killed or wounded in Vietnam, awarded 47 Medals of Honor, 362 Navy Crosses, and 2,592 Silver Star Medals for service in that war. In the Gulf War, out of a force of more than 300,000 soldiers, no Medals of Honor were awarded, nor were any Army Distinguished Service Crosses awarded. Two airmen won Air Force Distinguished Service Crosses, and two Marines won Navy Crosses. One hundred thirty-six Silver Stars were awarded. The only Medals of Honor earned in post-Vietnam combat were awarded to two soldiers who died while defending the crew of a downed Black Hawk helicopter in the Battle of Mogadishu, Somalia, in 1993.[29]

What is a Purple Heart?

A Purple Heart is earned by being wounded or killed in combat. The first Purple Hearts were awarded for valor by General George Washington in 1782. It is the oldest U.S. military decoration.[30]

How do I receive a combat decoration?

Someone must observe your bravery, write a description of your feat in battle, and recommend a citation. Someone in your theater of operations may be able to approve your citation, depending on the decoration. If not, the recommendation must be approved by the Pentagon.[31]

Can I be decorated if I die?

Awards are often given posthumously. More than half of the approximately 1,000 Medals of Honor awarded in the twentieth century were given to men who died earning them.[32]

Will I feel like my contributions have been recognized?

You should. Commanders have been taught to give positive feedback. Your unit may also receive public attention, especially in the media or in parades held after the war. However, some who participated in recent deployments have said that when their units received no television coverage, "We might as well not have been here."[33]

Will I feel close to others in my unit?

Almost definitely. You will communicate with your unit throughout a battle. You will undergo combat as a team. You will survive by working together. After combat you and your comrades will feel a strong bond. Every engagement will reinforce this bond.[34]

How will we communicate during battle?

When the enemy is nearby you may use flashing lights and hand signals. Otherwise you will use handheld and backpack radios. You will not often use voice commands to communicate with your unit during combat. These commands could be misunderstood in the noise of battle.[35]

Will someone rescue me if I am wounded?

Probably. According to the rules of engagement by which most countries' armies abide, medics wearing the sign of the International Committee of the Red Cross are not to be shot. The U.S. military has a sophisticated battlefield medical capability, including ranks of combat lifesavers (Army) and corpsmen (Navy and Marines) who provide battlefield care when medics are not available.[36]

What should I do if a comrade is wounded?

Your orders are to continue to fight if a comrade is wounded. Many ignore these orders. You will have been trained in basic first aid. This may be enough to save your comrade's life. A human being can suffer brain damage in as little as four minutes if he or she stops breathing. If more extensive care is required, call for a medic or corpsman.[37]

How will I feel if someone in my unit is killed?

It will affect you deeply. Gulf War veterans who lost a comrade ranked this as the most stressful incident of the war, worse than being attacked by enemy artillery, being wounded, or having a commander killed or wounded. You may feel guilty for surviving. You may wonder if you could have done more to prevent your comrade's death.[38]

What will the battle environment feel like?

You will most likely be subject to loud noise and vibration as well as a lack of oxygen, choking fumes, chemicals, skin irritants, bright light, and haze. You may be carrying heavy packs and weapons over unstable or uneven ground while being fired upon. You may be wet or very cold or very hot.[39]

Where will I likely be fighting?

Increasingly in urban areas. As populations moved to urban centers following World War II, so have the battles. Fighting in urban areas makes America's technological superiority less effective.[40]

How will fighting in urban areas affect my unit's tactics?

The density of urban areas and the presence of noncombatants create many obstacles. It is harder to identify specific targets. Most military maps for urban areas do not show man-made features in enough detail to support tactical operations. Combat in urban environments requires many soldiers. There are often heavier casualties.[41]

Are there less vulnerable ways to navigate an urban area?

You may use sewer or subway tunnels to maneuver throughout the city. The darkness and tight quarters make fighting in tunnels very difficult.[42]

What buildings am I forbidden to target?

Churches, synagogues, mosques, schools, hospitals, universities, museums, and historic monuments should not be targeted. You will, however, be permitted to attack or destroy these buildings if they are being used by the enemy for military purposes.[43]

Can I enter or destroy a civilian house?

The destruction, demolition, or occupation of houses is permissible if it is a matter of military necessity. For example, it is permissible to demolish a house to obtain a clear line of fire at the enemy. It is not permissible to demolish a house as an act of reprisal.[44]

How will fighting in a desert affect my combat tactics?

It will be hard to conceal yourself. Desert terrain is open and uniform. It is easily disturbed by vehicle tracks. Vehicle movement produces dust and gas fumes that can be seen easily. Sound and light can be detected at great distances. Navigation is hard because of limited landmarks. It is more difficult to evade air attacks. Sandstorms can erode and clog equipment.[45]

How will fighting in a jungle affect my combat tactics?

You will have a harder time spotting the enemy. Ground-level visibility in most jungles is limited to about 50 meters. Visibility can diminish to 2 to 5 meters in especially thick growth. Driving vehicles is difficult. Trees and bushes provide excellent opportunities for ambush. The enemy may have extensive tunnel and bunker networks. Visibility is limited from the air.[46]

How will fighting in the mountains affect my combat tactics?

In thin air everything takes more energy. You will need to eat more, although you may lose weight despite the extra calories. Black Hawk helicopters and other aircraft have performance limitations at high altitudes and may not be available. FM radio communications may be ineffective due to the high altitude and operating distances.[47]

How will fighting at night affect my combat skills?

As the air cools, radar and radio signals have a hard time traveling. Visibility decreases. With night-vision glasses you cannot see color. Basic tasks, such as patrolling, are more difficult and dangerous. Speed is sacrificed for accuracy. Fatigue, fear, feelings of isolation, and loss of confidence may increase.[48]

Does the U.S. military prefer to fight at night?

Yes. The U.S. often uses inclement weather or darkness to attack. The U.S. military possesses a wide range of night-vision capabilities, more than most enemy armed forces.[49]

Will I fight well-trained soldiers?

Not necessarily. The enemies in the future will probably be guerrillas and militia fighters who do not abide by the accepted rules of war.[50]

What if the enemy tries to surrender?

You are supposed to stop shooting. Killing or wounding an enemy who is trying to surrender is a serious breach of the Laws of War. They are supposed to come out with their hands up, wave a white flag, put down weapons, or in some way demonstrate surrender. However, they may not want to surrender fully. They may want a temporary truce. They may also be trying to get closer to your position to launch an attack, observe your defenses, or buy time to shift forces. It is illegal to use a surrender attempt in this way. Some of the first American casualties in the Iraqi War were due to fake surrenders from Iraqi forces. They waved a white flag and then opened fire.[51]

Who can I not shoot?

In addition to civilians, you may not shoot prisoners of war, chaplains, medical personnel, or military personnel removed from combat, such as shipwreck victims or pilots parachuting from damaged planes. In the heat of battle, however, you might err on the side of shooting too many people rather than too few.[52]

Should I trust civilians?

Not necessarily. Civilians often have information about the enemy, local terrain, and weather, but you cannot always rely on the information because you will not know their allegiances.[53]

Must I always avoid killing civilians?

No. You may cause civilian casualties if you are attacking a legitimate target. You may be forced to shoot an enemy if he or she is using civilians as human shields. Civilians are not combatants and are not lawful targets unless they take part in the hostilities against you and are a threat to you.[54]

What if an officer gives me a command that I believe is illegal?

You must refuse to execute it.[55]

Will I be able to resist killing civilians if my commanding officer orders me to?

Under direct but unlawful orders, and if your leader is killing civilians himself, you will find it hard to resist. Lieutenant Colonel (Ret.) Dave Grossman wrote of an incident in the Vietnam War: "When Lieutenant Calley first ordered his men to kill a group of women and children in the village of My Lai, he said, 'You know what to do with them,' and left. When he came back he asked, 'Why haven't you killed them?' The soldier he confronted said, 'I didn't think you wanted us to kill them.' 'No,' Calley responded, 'I want them dead,' and proceeded to fire at

Calley responded, 'I want them dead,' and proceeded to fire at them himself. Only then was he able to get his soldiers to start shooting in this extraordinary circumstance in which the soldiers' resistance to killing was, understandably, very high."[56]

What if an officer gives me a command that I believe will get me killed?

Refusal to follow a lawful order in combat can result in a court-martial.[57]

If I am a high-ranking officer will I be more likely to survive?

Maybe. During 10 years of war in Vietnam, one general and eight full colonels died in combat. As one study commissioned by the military concluded, "In Vietnam . . . the officer corps simply did not die in sufficient numbers or in the presence of their men often enough."[58]

Do troops ever kill their own officers?

Troops sometimes attempt to kill officers whose recklessness or incompetence might threaten the lives of those in the units they command. The term "fragging"—attempted assassination of an officer by his own troops—came into use during the Vietnam War. At least 600 officers were fragged by their own troops in Vietnam. The deaths of an additional 1,400 officers could not be explained.[59]

How dangerous is friendly fire?

Friendly fire may have been responsible for as many as 15 percent of all American casualties during the last century. During the World War II Allied invasion of the Aleutian island of Kiska, friendly fire was responsible for 28 men killed in action and 50 men wounded in action, even though all Japanese forces had previously evacuated the island. Friendly fire accounted for 24 percent of those killed in action and 15 percent of those wounded in action in the Gulf War.[60]

Where am I most vulnerable to friendly fire?

Most friendly fire injuries in recent wars have occurred because tanks and vehicles were improperly targeted. Seventy-seven percent of all combat vehicles lost in the Gulf War were destroyed by friendly fire.[61]

How will I feel when combat ends?

You may feel exhilaration at being alive. You may feel strong emotion (positive or negative) depending on how the battle went. You may remain energized until shortly after the enemy threat has dissipated. Once the threat appears to be gone, you will become extremely fatigued. Your body will stop producing adrenaline. Your muscles will start to unclench from the exertion of combat. Your pack may begin to feel extremely heavy. A cunning enemy will attack with reserve units when the "victor" relaxes.[62]

What are the chances I will have a negative reaction to combat?

Almost one in three. During and immediately after combat about 15 to 30 percent of soldiers experience "combat stress reaction." This condition may include extreme sensitivity to sound, stuttering, dissociation, loss of control, nausea, paranoid responses, disorientation, and confusion. You may find yourself shaking or curled up in a fetal position. If it does not happen to you it may happen to someone near you.[63]

What is combat stress?

Combat stress, also known as battle fatigue, is a common reaction to the imminent and inescapable threat of serious personal injury or death. Signs of combat stress can appear long after battle. These include trembling, jumpiness, cold sweats, dizziness, vomiting, diarrhea, and a "thousand-yard stare." You may have difficulty speaking or thinking, along with nightmares, shaking, trembling, or an inability to see, hear, feel, or speak. You may not be able to use your hands, arms, or legs. You may be indifferent to danger. You may experience severe stuttering, or you may see and hear things that do not exist.[64]

How will I be treated if I develop combat stress?

You may have your weapon confiscated and be physically restrained. You will be taken off the front lines but treated within range of enemy artillery. Removing people from battlefields makes it less likely they will be able to return to fight. Sixty-five to 85 percent of combat stress casualties return to combat within one to three days. Fifteen to 20 percent return in one to two weeks. Five to 10 percent of those removed from the field of battle due to combat stress never recover.[65]

What will my treatment involve?

Rest, recuperation, and confidence-building talks. You will probably be visited by a member of your unit to remind you that you are not far from the field of battle. You will be told that you are reacting normally to combat stress and that you are a warrior, not a patient. You may be given drugs to help you stay alert. You will not receive psychotherapy.[66]

What should I do if someone in my unit has a severe stress reaction?

Try to calm him or her down. Reassure your comrade. Get the person to talk about what happened. Explain that combat stress is a normal response to the abnormal situation of war.[67]

Can I be a combat stress casualty if I am not in battle?

Yes. Members of service units and reservists are more vulnerable to stress. Many reserve units are mobilized shortly before deploying. This limits the bonding and support they can offer one another.[68]

What negative behaviors can arise as a consequence of combat stress?

You may mutilate the enemy dead. You may rape, torture or kill noncombatants or prisoners. You may kill animals or fight with your comrades. You may abuse alcohol or drugs. You may be reckless, have a lack of discipline, and engage in looting or pillaging. You may refuse treatment for a disease or injury. You may refuse to fight. You may wound yourself, or threaten or kill officers. You may go absent without leave or desert.[69]

What are the first signs of psychiatric collapse?

The first is fatigue. You become unsociable and overly irritable. You lose interest in all activities with comrades. You seek to avoid any activity involving physical or mental exertion. You become prone to crying fits or extreme anxiety or terror. You become hypersensitive to sound. You experience increased sweating and palpitations. These reactions set the stage for complete collapse. If you are forced to remain in combat for too long, psychiatric collapse is probably inevitable.[70]

How should I cope with stress?

Deep breathing, muscle relaxation, and cognitive exercises such as positive thinking and visualization may help.[71]

Will drugs aid me in combat?

Amphetamines and caffeine will increase your alertness. During the Gulf War 57 percent of Air Force pilots used stimulants at least once. Sixty-one percent said the stimulants were essential to their mission's success. Seventy-one percent of

Vietnam veterans said that many servicemen entered combat after using marijuana or harder drugs.[72]

Will alcohol help me in combat?
No. The precision and technical skill required in modern warfare is not aided by alcohol. During World War I many soldiers went into battle "less than sober, if not fighting drunk." This is rarely the case in the modern American army.[73]

What is a "combat high"?
Combat veteran Jack Thompson wrote that "combat addiction . . . is caused when, during a firefight, the body releases a large amount of adrenaline into your system and you get what is referred to as a 'combat high.' This combat high is like getting an injection of morphine—you float around, laughing, joking, having a great time, totally oblivious to the dangers around you. The experience is very intense if you live to tell about it. Problems arise when you begin to want another fix of combat, and another, and another, and before you know it, you're hooked. As with heroin or cocaine addiction, combat addiction will surely get you killed. And like any addict, you get desperate and will do anything to get your fix."[74]

What will I think about in combat?
You will be aware of the immediate danger, but your other thoughts may wander. You will probably be unable to focus in combat lulls. Your military training, based on repetition and muscle memory, should help you perform your task. You may become fixated on the danger you face. You may worry about death. You may also think about home.[75]

What will happen to me following particularly horrible sights, sounds, or smells?
You may experience temporary blindness, deafness, or an

inability to smell. These are known as "hysterical" reactions. They help you cope with stress. Your nose, ears, and eyes function, but because of the stress your brain cannot process the incoming data.[76]

How common are mental disorders arising from combat?

There was a greater chance of becoming a psychiatric casualty than of being killed by enemy fire in every major war during the twentieth century. From 1942 through 1945 in the European theater there was one psychiatric casualty for every three men wounded in action. In all, 504,000 men were lost from America's fighting forces in World War II due to psychiatric collapse—enough to man 50 divisions. According to some reports, more Vietnam veterans have committed suicide since the war than were killed during it. Of the 3.5 million Vietnam veterans, an estimated 500,000 to 1.5 million have been affected by psychiatric disorders.[77]

How long can I remain in sustained combat?

The longer you stay in combat, the greater the chance you will become a psychiatric casualty. After approximately 25 days in battle the emotional and physical stress will have exhausted most combatants' reserves.[78]

What will prolonged exposure to combat do to me?

In World War II it was determined that after 60 days of continuous combat, 98 percent of all those who survive will have become psychiatric casualties. The common trait among the 2 percent who were able to endure sustained combat was a predisposition toward "aggressive psychopathic personalities." Lieutenant Colonel (Ret.) Dave Grossman wrote: "It is not too far from the mark to observe that there is something about continuous, inescapable combat which will drive 98 percent of all men insane, and the other 2 percent were crazy when they got there."[79]

Chapter 7

IMPRISONMENT, TORTURE, AND RAPE

What happens if I am taken prisoner?

During the first 24 hours, you will probably experience shock and trauma, including an overwhelming fear of death. You will try to take control of your emotions, but you will not be able to think clearly. After 24 or 48 hours, you will begin to calm down. You will probably experience hope that you will survive, though the fear of death will be omnipresent. You may experience physical symptoms ranging from headaches to excessive urination. After 48 hours, if you have not been tortured, you will probably start to adapt to the situation. In captivity, those with the strongest will to survive are the most likely to do so. They make a conscious decision to live within a matter of days or weeks after capture.[1]

Will I be ashamed if I am captured?

You may feel shame, and have feelings of helplessness, abandonment, guilt, and depression, as well as loss of confidence and self-control.[2]

What does the military say I should do if I am taken prisoner?

Do not give any information other than your name, rank, date of birth, and Social Security number. According to the U.S. Military Code of Conduct, you must try to escape and to help others escape. You must not promise your captors you will not try to escape.[3]

How will I be treated if I am captured?

You may be deprived of food and medical care, physically or sexually abused, and interrogated for seemingly endless periods. POW experiences differ based on the culture of their captors.[4]

What is the best way to survive captivity?

Some prisoners become engrossed in trivial activities and the minor events of daily life. They adhere to daily rituals and avoid focusing on the situation. Captives who are strongly committed to a cause or ideology, and have the strongest will to live, are most likely to survive long, stressful periods of captivity. Also crucial is group support and communication with others, as well as faith and loyalty to fellow prisoners. One Vietnam POW credited the society of fellow captives and their intense unity and confidence for his survival. One POW in World War II found great relief in remembering good times with friends and using his imagination to visualize being somewhere else.[5]

What happens to my salary if I am captured?

You will continue to be paid for as long as you are a POW. Your income may be put into a trust or made available to your family.[6]

What will happen to me if I collaborate with or help my captors?

A volunteer informer or collaborator is considered a traitor to fellow prisoners and country, according to the Code of Conduct for Members of the Armed Forces of the United States. After you are freed, you will be subject to punishment. However, American POWs held in Vietnam found it impossible to adhere exactly to the code. This was a source of guilt for some of these men.[7]

Will I develop a friendship with my captors?

Maybe. If, after 48 hours of captivity, no form of torture has been implemented, POWs often find that they have few bad feelings toward their captors. In some cases, the captors also develop positive feelings toward their captives. A captor-hostage bond, however, usually requires compassionate treatment alternating with threats of death and torture.[8]

Will I be able to stay in shape if I am a prisoner?

Possibly. One POW from the Vietnam War did 400 push-ups a day, even with leg irons on, but some Vietnam POWs weighed only 90 pounds when they were released from captivity. Most were undernourished and had suffered severe physical deprivation. Many POWs in Japan during World War II were starved, forced to work, and denied exercise privileges.[9]

Will I be able to get mail or messages from home if I am a prisoner?

Probably not, although the protocols of the Geneva Conventions state that POWs should be allowed to send and receive mail.[10]

How many prisoners of war escape or are rescued?

That depends on the war. Of the 801 American POWs captured during the Vietnam War, 36 escaped and returned to the

U.S. Rescues are much less likely. Private First Class Jessica Lynch, rescued from Iraqi captors on April 3, 2003, was the first American POW rescued from enemy forces since World War II.[11]

Can I resist interrogation?

Although enemy interrogation sessions may be harsh and cruel, it may be possible to resist initially.[12]

Can I withstand torture?

Not past a certain point, though that point varies. The same military regulations that urge you to remain silent concede that it is "very unlikely that you will be able to prevent a skilled enemy interrogator, using all available psychological and physical methods of coercion, from forcing you to comply at least a little with his demands."[13]

How do interrogators make captured soldiers talk?

Captors use a wide range of physical and psychological torture tactics to elicit information. In Kindu, Democratic Republic of the Congo, in 1999, combatants reportedly boasted that they had intentionally infected their rape victims with HIV. In Sri Lanka in the last 13 years, revolutionary forces (the Liberation Tigers of Tamil Eelam) have beaten prisoners while hanging them from their feet, forced them to inhale chili fumes, inserted pins under their fingernails, and burned them with heated metal rods.[14]

What are the most common forms of physical torture?

Some of the most common include use of electric shocks, long beatings (especially of the genitals and soles of the feet), violent sexual assault and rape, burning, choking, and immersion in excrement.[15]

What are the most common forms of psychological torture?

Some methods include depriving captives of sound, sleep, light, or darkness, threatening to kill or mutilate the captive or his loved ones, and staging mock executions.[16]

What is the most effective form of torture?

Many consider threats to people close to the prisoner, mock executions, and rape and other forms of sexual assault to be most effective at causing mental and physical trauma.[17]

Who invented torture?

Torture was used to elicit truth in cases of serious crime in ancient Greece and the Roman Empire. It was used on slaves, foreigners, and others who had no legal status, but was later employed on other segments of the population. It then disappeared from Europe until the twelfth century. In the mid-eighteenth-century, torture as part of the legal process was abolished in Europe, but it reappeared during World War II, when it was widely used in German-occupied territories. Though the 1948 Universal Declaration of Human Rights prohibits torture, the practice persists today.[18]

How common is torture in wartime?

Torture is widely used as a means of waging war. Over the past 10 years, some of the conflicts in which torture has been used include those in Bosnia, Algeria, the Democratic Republic of the Congo, Colombia, and Sri Lanka.[19]

What percentage of captured soldiers are tortured?

Precise statistics on the prevalence of torture of prisoners are not available. Part of the nature of torturous acts is that they are not committed in the presence of independent witnesses. All of the 21 American POWs who were held captive by Iraq during the Gulf War reported being beaten with rubber hoses, boards, sticks, leather straps, and hammers; shocked with cattle prods; threatened with dismemberment; deprived of food; and coerced into making videotapes. At least 40 percent of the POWs who returned from Vietnam in 1973 underwent torture.[20]

Are female POWs raped?

They may be. Of the two female POWs in the Gulf War, one was sexually abused, and one was raped.[21]

Why will I be tortured?

Your captors want military information and statements that can be used for intelligence or propaganda.[22]

Does torture work?

Most people break under torture, confessing or giving information. Torture also dehumanizes, humiliates, and irreparably damages victims both physically and mentally.[23]

How many of those who are tortured give information?

Most. You will probably do what your captors say. You will be overwhelmed with feelings of helplessness and fears that captivity may be long. Many prisoners die in captivity, but very few can withstand torture long enough to die of torture itself. Almost all of the American POWs who returned to the U.S. from Vietnam in 1973 reported that they had been forced to do or say things against their will.[24]

Do American military interrogators torture prisoners?

Possibly, though they are not supposed to. American intelligence personnel have been suspected of torturing prisoners, most recently in Afghanistan. There, noncooperative captives were reportedly kept standing or kneeling for hours, in black hoods or spray-painted goggles. They were restrained in awkward, painful positions, and deprived of sleep and darkness. Some of the least cooperative were handed to foreign intelligence services known for using harsher means.[25]

How long do torture sessions last?

This varies widely. Torture can last for hours, days, or even weeks and months. In one case of prolonged psychological torture, a POW in Vietnam was kept in solitary confinement for four of his nearly eight years as a POW.[26]

Is information gleaned through torture credible?

No. Most people will do or say anything to stop torture.[27]

What will happen if I survive my torture and imprisonment?

Nightmares, memory problems, depression, paranoia, and an inability to connect with others are common, even years after torture. Symptoms are significantly more severe among those who were subjected to mock execution during their confinement. Chronic physical symptoms can persist as well, including respiratory infections, ulcers, and impairment of vision.[28]

Is rape common in war?

Yes. In Kosovo, approximately 20,000 women were raped between 1992 and 1994. In Rwanda, between 250,000 and 500,000 women were raped during the 1994 genocide. In Bangladesh, at least 200,000 women were raped at the hands of West Pakistani troops in the conflict that began in 1971. In Kuwait, 5,000 women were raped and tortured during the Iraqi occupation of 1990.[29]

Is rape considered a war crime?

Yes, though it has rarely been taken as seriously as others. According to the United Nations, "Rape remains the least condemned war crime." It was not until 1993 that rape was declared a crime against humanity—an inhumane act that is part of a systematic attack against a civilian population.[30]

Why are so many women raped in war?

Rape is used as a weapon. Enemy women are sometimes raped to force them to bear children or contract disease. Women are kidnapped and used as sexual slaves to service troops, as well as to cook for them and carry their loads from camp to camp. Women are also raped as a form of interrogation. These are all considered war crimes.[31]

Why is rape an effective weapon?

Rape terrorizes civilian populations. It can cause civilians to flee, which can make it easier to establish military control. It can make the rapists feel dominant, the victims feel ashamed, and the rival forces feel humiliated.[32]

What are the effects of rape upon victims?

The physical consequences of sexual violence include injury, unwanted pregnancies, sexual dysfunction, and HIV/AIDS. Many victims of sexual assault never psychologically recover. Aftereffects can include anxiety, post-traumatic stress disorders, depression, and suicide. When women are impregnated through rape, the trauma is greatly increased. Even those who have the choice to abort face the health risks and trauma of the procedure.[33]

What is the incidence of rape in the U.S. military?

In peacetime, male U.S. military personnel are less likely to commit rape than are male civilians of the same age. In the heightened aggression of combat, all violent acts are more common, including rape. In March and April 1945, during World War II, the rape rate for U.S. Army forces in the European theater of operations was 3.66 times the U.S. male civilian rate.[34]

Chapter 8

DYING

How will I die?

Most combat wounds result in the loss of too much blood. Had you made it to old age, you might have had enough blood, but a heart too weak to pump it, or arteries too clogged to allow it to travel around your body. The end result is the same: your brain stops functioning because the lack of blood cuts off its only source of oxygen.[1]

Is blood loss the only way I can die during a war?

No, just the most common. Even if you have enough blood, you may not be able to get enough oxygen into it if your throat is crushed, or your lung is punctured. Additionally, your brain can stop functioning if you are struck or shot in the head. Or you could die slowly from an infected wound.[2]

How long will it take me to die if I am wounded?

It depends on how long it takes you to lose enough blood. If you are a 170-pound man, the loss of eight pints of blood is enough to stop your heart. If you are a 130-pound woman, six pints is enough. If you tear a major blood vessel, you can lose this much blood in less than one minute. A tear or hole in a blood-filled organ like the liver or spleen may cause you to bleed to death over the course of several hours.[3]

What does it feel like to die?

You will be conscious for part of it. According to people who have been clinically dead and then resuscitated, you will feel your consciousness swiftly wind down. It will not flip from on to off, like a light, but rather will gradually disappear, like a match burning out.[4]

Could I be resuscitated?

If you lose a massive amount of blood, your heart will stop beating. Your breathing and brain activity will stop. Your cells will not die immediately. If you are resuscitated and receive a blood transfusion within four minutes you may live.[5]

Will I feel pain when I die?

Possibly not. When you are wounded, your body may release endorphins to raise your pain threshold. However, the pain may be too great for the endorphins to handle, in which case you will feel the pain of being wounded.[6]

Will I know I am dying?

Probably not. Or, more accurately, if you are conscious enough to think you might be dying, you will probably survive. Medical support for the American military is very effective. If you do not die within the first hour of being wounded, you will probably live to recover. Terminally ill patients are sometimes uncannily able to predict the hour of their death, but those who die from sudden traumas like gunshot wounds have no such ability.[7]

What happens to my body and bodily functions as I die?

Your heart will start beating faster to compensate for the blood loss. It will send what blood is left to the body more quickly. You will probably also hyperventilate to get oxygen into your remaining blood.

Eventually, you will go into a coma. Your cerebral cortex, the part of your brain used for thought and emotion, will die first. The lower parts of the brain, such as the brain stem, will live longer, allowing respiration, digestion, and circulation to continue. Finally, your near-empty heart will stop altogether.

You may stop breathing. You may have a series of gasps. Your chest or shoulders may heave once or twice. There may be a brief, full-body convulsion. You will go through "death agonies." These are the random spasms of muscles caused by highly acidic blood in a dying body. If this spasming takes place in the muscles in your voice box, it will produce a last gasp sometimes called a "death rattle." Finally, your muscles, including your anal sphincter, will relax. Your pupils will dilate completely.[8]

What will my last words be?

Those who die in combat often call for their mothers. From one account of Vietnam: "I didn't really speak the language. I could understand a few phrases, though. One day during a firefight, for the first time in my life, I heard the cries of the Vietnamese wounded, and I understood them. When someone gets wounded, they call out for their mothers, their wives, their girlfriends. There I was listening to the VC cry for the same things."[9]

Will I die alone?

Dying alone is a common fear. Nobody wants it to happen. If possible, your fellow soldiers will not let it happen to you.[10]

Will I be scared when I die?

Possibly not. The endorphins your brain pumps into your body to heighten your resistance to pain may also affect your mood, even if you know that you are badly hurt. This may be

corpses are found with surprised or peaceful ex-
...their faces.[11]

What will my body look like after I die?

Your face will lose its color a minute after your heartbeat stops. Your eyes will lose their shine after about five minutes. They will look as if they have a gray film over them. Your eyeballs will flatten slightly. Your body will have the flaccid feel of a slab of meat.[12]

Will I be frozen in the position in which I die?

Only if you are left there for a few hours. Soon after you die, your muscles will begin to contract, producing rigor mortis. It will happen first in your face, neck, hands, and feet. You can be straightened out after rigor mortis has set, but only with effort. About 48 hours after your death, your body will begin to lose its stiffness due to bacterial decay.[13]

What will happen to my body after I die?

A doctor will pronounce you dead while you are still in the field. Your body will be put on a stretcher and taken to a collection site. You will be laid out on a tarp with others who died in battle. The collection site, if possible, will be out of sight of the wounded and fresh replacements. Your personal effects will be removed from your pockets. These effects will be placed in a plastic bag and marked with your name, date of birth, and Social Security number. Your weapon, ammunition, and any other government property will be set aside for reuse.[14]

Will my body be recovered from combat?

Probably. The U.S. military tries to recover its dead. However, if you are killed over water, or at the heart of an explosion, your remains may not be recoverable. Geographical, climatic, or political conditions may also make recovery of your remains too difficult. The enemy may also take your body.[15]

Will the enemy mutilate my dead body?

Maybe. Mutilating enemy dead is a violation of the general laws of warfare, but it happens. [16]

Will I be buried by my enemy?

Maybe. Especially in warm climates, dead bodies must be buried promptly to prevent disease. If you die in an area the enemy wants to continue to use, you may be buried. International treaties require that your remains be collected, identified, and disposed of in a marked, individual grave, and that the U.S. government be provided with the cause of your death and location of your grave. However, despite treaties, your body may be thrown in a mass grave, bartered for prisoners of war, or never found.[17]

Will the enemy steal my possessions after I am dead?

Probably. The enemy will go through your pockets to look for intelligence information. He will also take anything, including your weapon, that helps him fight more effectively.[18]

Will my body be treated with respect?

Yes. However, many of those who view your body will see it as an object; no longer human. Humor and callousness help them focus on their job. This may be especially true for mortuary affairs personnel, who tend to suffer more if they learn too much about the lives of the people whose bodies they handle.[19]

How will my family be informed of my death?

Your family will be notified in person by a casualty notification officer of equal or greater rank than yourself who will arrive in a full dress uniform. The officer will have as much information as is available about the circumstances of your death and the current disposition of your remains. The officer will have been instructed not to physically touch your family in any manner unless they suffer shock or faint. The officer will summon medical assistance immediately for your family if necessary.[20]

How will I be prepared for burial?

You will be washed. Your fingernails will be trimmed. Your face will be shaved if you are a man. Your mouth will be closed. Any wounds will be sutured or sealed to prevent leakage. Swollen or distorted features will be restored. Your body orifices will be chemically disinfected and packed with cotton. Maggots and other insect larvae will be destroyed. Their breeding sites will be treated with an insecticide. If it is present, gas will be removed from your head, chest, and abdomen. Your body will be drained of natural fluids and filled with preservatives. If your remains are viewable but your hands are mutilated, they will be wrapped in gauze or surgical gloves, followed by white military gloves.[21]

What if my remains are too damaged to be presentable?

If your remains cannot be clothed, they will be covered with cotton strips, and wrapped in plastic. A white cotton sheet will be wrapped around your remains, followed by a blanket. The blanket will have as few creases in it as possible. It will be secured with large safety pins placed no more than eight inches apart.[22]

Can I donate my organs if I die in combat?

Probably not. The circumstances of your death will make it difficult to harvest and preserve your organs. However, if you live long enough to be evacuated to a major medical center, and you make your desire to be a donor known before you die, an attempt will be made to honor your wishes.[23]

What will happen to my personal effects?

Personal effects found on your body will be inventoried at the first mortuary affairs collection point. When they are no longer required for identification purposes, your effects will be evacuated to the personal effects depot. They will be packed for shipment, with each package marked "Effects of Deceased Person" and bearing your name, grade, Social Security number, and organization.[24]

Who will receive my personal effects?

Only one person may be designated to receive your personal effects. This person will be determined through an examination of your personal records. The order of precedence is spouse, child, parent, sibling, other blood relative, foster parent or stepparent, or a person named as a beneficiary in your will. Sentimental items such as wedding bands, religious medals, and lockets will be released in time to be available for your funeral.[25]

What if there is something in my personal effects that I do not want sent home?

It will probably be removed. The officer in charge will use common sense in deciding what should be sent home. He or she will remove anything that might cause your next of kin embarrassment or added sorrow, including anything obscene, unsanitary, mutilated, burned, or bloodstained. Items such as letters, papers, photographs, and videotapes will be screened.[26]

Will my remains receive a military escort home?

Yes. Because you were killed in combat, your body is eligible for a military escort. The escort, preferably from your service branch and of your rank or higher, will travel with your body from the battlefield mortuary back to the United States to your family's chosen cemetery.[27]

How soon after I die will I be buried?

It will probably take two to four weeks. During wartime, it can take ten days or more for your body to be collected from the field, evacuated to a mortuary, processed, and sent back to the U.S. Arranging burial in a national cemetery takes an average of five to seven days.[28]

Where will I be buried?

All veterans can be buried free of charge at one of 60 national cemeteries maintained by the Department of Veterans Affairs. There are a total of 120 national cemeteries in the U.S., but 60 of them will be closed to new burials by the end of 2003. However, 24 of these are open to veterans who are willing to be cremated. If you are related to someone who is already buried at one of the 60 closed cemeteries, you are allowed to be buried in his or her plot.[29]

Can I be buried at Arlington National Cemetery?

Yes. Since you were killed during active duty, you are eligible to be buried at Arlington. If you had not been killed while serving, you would have to have a Purple Heart, or a Silver Star or higher, to be buried there. Of the almost 3 million veterans who are buried in military cemeteries, 200,000 are at Arlington.[30]

What will my funeral be like?

Your funeral will be run by a military chaplain provided by the cemetery, unless your family or the funeral home chooses to provide clergy. Your family may also request military honors for your funeral. The honors will be provided by your service branch, and will include body bearers (pall bearers), a firing party, and a bugler or a recording of Taps. The U.S. government pays for your body's transportation, religious services, grave site, and other burial expenses. It provides a free tombstone.[31]

Will I receive a 21-gun salute?

Yes. You will receive a rifle volley of three volleys from seven rifles. Your family, if it requests them, may be allowed to keep the cartridges of the blanks that are fired.[32]

What will my tombstone say?

Your tombstone will include your name, branch of service, and year of birth and death, in that order. Space permitting, you may also include your rank, the war in which you died, complete dates of your birth and death, military awards, military organizations, and civilian affiliations. You can also include one of 32 approved "symbols of belief" to commemorate your religious faith or atheism. Your tombstone can also include a nickname or term of endearment, as long as it is tasteful and is approved by the Department of Veterans Affairs. You are eligible for this free tombstone even if you choose to be buried in a civilian cemetery.[33]

If I am buried in a national cemetery, can my spouse be buried with me?

Yes. You may leave space on your tombstone for the inscription of his or her information. However, if your spouse remarries after your death, and then dies while married to somebody else, he or she cannot be buried with you. If your spouse's new marriage ends before your spouse's death, he or she is again eligible to be buried with you.[34]

Will people visit my grave?

In 2002, the 3 million veteran graves in national cemeteries had almost 13 million visitors. Four million of these visitors came to Arlington to pay their respects at the graves of the approximately 200,000 soldiers buried there. If you choose not to be buried at Arlington, you can probably be buried close to your family. Approximately three out of four veterans have access to a national cemetery within 75 miles of their last U.S. address.[35]

What will my family receive to remember me by?

Your family will receive the U.S. flag that was used to drape your coffin.[36]

What are the likely effects on my child if I die?

Your child may develop serious problems in school. He or she may become angry with playmates, or express anger toward you and criticize you. Children who have lost a parent tend to be more submissive, dependent, and introverted than children who have living parents. They suffer a higher incidence of maladjustment and emotional disturbance, including thoughts of suicide. They are also more likely to participate in delinquent and criminal behavior. They tend to perform less well in school and in tests of cognitive functioning. Physical and mental illness occurs more frequently in the adult lives of people who suffered bereavement in their childhood.[37]

How will my spouse react to my death?

Your spouse will feel overwhelmed and anguished. He or she may cry ceaselessly, experience numbness, or be unable to move. Physical symptoms of aches, pains, poor appetite, loss of stamina, headaches, and dizziness may linger for weeks or months. Sleep disturbance is common. Grief may interfere with his or her ability to care for the emotional needs of your children. Your spouse may feel angry with you for leaving him or her alone to raise your children. The months after the funeral, when relatives, neighbors, and colleagues return back to their routine, will be the most difficult for him or her. It takes a year in most cases to learn to cope with the loss.[38]

How will my parents cope with my death?

Your death will be one of the most traumatic experiences your parents will endure. They will initially feel numbness and shock. They may deny your death. They will probably be overwhelmed by feelings of anger, guilt, rage and frustration. They may need assistance in deciding whom to notify about your death and how to arrange your funeral. Their numbness will gradually give way to an intense grief. This period will be painful and depressing. It will be characterized by a loss of appetite, insomnia, irritability, muscular aches, and digestive problems. Your parents may use alcohol or drugs to ease their grief. Gradually they will return to those activities they enjoyed prior to your death, but most parents say they never fully recover from the death of a child.[30]

Chapter 9

AFTER THE WAR

Will I want to go home?

Yes. Studies have shown repeatedly that one of the most important goals of those who fight is "to go home."[1]

Should I come straight home?

No. While the military makes it possible to be home 48 hours after being released from service, an abrupt transition can be unhealthy. Your unit should take time to discuss what happened during the war. It should perform appropriate ceremonies or rituals. You should have some equivalent of the historical "long march home" in which you have the time to process your war experience before you return to civilian life.[2]

Will I come home when I expect to?

Maybe not. False rumors of a rotation date might spread through your unit. Your actual date of return might change unexpectedly. Your unit might not return together—others might leave days before you.[3]

What will I worry about before I come home?

You will worry about whether your spouse missed you and was faithful. You will worry about how your children will react when they see you and live with you again. You will wonder if they have been treated well while you were away. You will worry that your role in the family will change. You will wonder how your spouse has handled the family's finances. You will worry about whether your friends will still be there for you and whether they have changed. You will worry that you have lost valuable time that you will not be able to make up. You will worry that you will be deployed again.[4]

What will homecoming be like?

Your family will rush to you. You will embrace and kiss your spouse. Your unit will come to attention for one last time. Your commander will praise you. You will turn in your weapons, retrieve your bag, and go home.[5]

Will I feel appreciated?

People will probably be friendly. You might not be satisfied. This will be due in part to the impossible fantasy of your homecoming you will have built up since the beginning of your deployment. After a parade or similar appreciation, many will feel their debt to you has been repaid. You will probably also feel that because American civilians have no direct experience of war, they cannot relate to what you went through. Fifty-eight percent of Vietnam veterans said people at home did not understand what they had been through during the war.[6]

If I serve in an unpopular war, will I be received angrily when I come home?

No, at least not by most people. Ninety-nine percent of veterans returning from Vietnam said they had a friendly reception from close friends and family, and 94 percent said they got a friendly reception from people their own age who had not served. Seventy-five percent of Vietnam-era veterans thought war protesters did not blame veterans for the war.[7]

Will I be spit on or harassed?

Probably not. Research indicates that the story of the returning Vietnam veteran spat upon by a protester at the airport may be an urban legend. Newspaper accounts from the war era do describe spitting incidents, but the spat-upon people are antiwar protesters. However, there are credible reports of hostility and violence toward men and women in uniform. Some Vietnam veterans reported discrimination from college and graduate school admissions offices. Others reported verbal abuse. This continues to the present day. In some states, assaulting or abusing a person because of membership in the military is a hate crime.[8]

Will people who did not see combat say they did?

Yes. One Vietnam veteran followed up on 1,700 news stories about combat-damaged veterans and found three-quarters of their subjects to be frauds—either never having seen combat, or never having served in the military.[9]

Will I want to leave the military after the war?

Probably not. Most who serve in today's armed forces think of the military as their career, and resent the fact that the force is reduced during peacetime.[10]

How will I feel when I get home?

You may have trouble adjusting. You may be easily startled by noise or sudden movement. You may have combat dreams or nightmares and trouble sleeping. You may be tired of routine and regimentation, be exhausted, and want to relax. It is common to feel bored, frustrated, and out of place.[11]

What will it be like to see my spouse again?

Happy, but awkward. Your spouse may resent you for having "abandoned" your family for months. Stay-at-home parents often report more stress than the deployed parents. Your spouse may seem more confident and independent. If you were the main decision maker in the house before you left, he or she has probably taken over that role, and may be reluctant to relinquish it.[12]

Will I have trouble having sex with my spouse?

Maybe. You may experience sexual problems, even if you serve in a short war. Some veterans report a "prostitute complex," in which their desire for sex has greatly increased since deployment. Physical or mental combat trauma also increases the risk of sexual problems. Most likely, you will be intimate physically, but not emotionally at first.[13]

How should I deal with my children?

Carefully. They might be anxious for a year or more after your return, fearful that you will leave again. They might be scared that you have come back to discipline them. They might be alienated if you take away privileges your spouse gave them while you were away.[14]

How will my children treat me?

A baby may cry more. A toddler may not recognize you and may act shy. A toddler may also forget his or her toilet training. A preschooler may be angry and demanding, acting out and wanting you to prove you are real. A child between 5 and 12 years old may feel inferior to you, and unworthy of your attention. Teenagers might want to hear about what you have done, or might rebel against your authority and ignore you.[15]

How long will the war affect me?

Maybe your whole life. In a 2001 survey of World War II and Korean War veterans aged 59 to 89, 19 percent showed significant psychological distress in relation to their war experiences. Many still had trouble discussing their experiences. Other studies have shown lingering effects of trauma in World War II veterans 50 years after the war, and one revealed effects persisting 75 years after World War I.[16]

What are the long-term consequences of combat stress?

There is a direct link between severe stress exposure and long-term health problems. Twenty years after their exposure to combat, Vietnam veterans showed a higher rate of circulatory, digestive, musculoskeletal, metabolic, nervous system, and respiratory problems. They were also at greater risk for some infectious diseases.[17]

What are some of the specific problems I might develop?

You are at a greater risk for drug-related disorders and alcoholism, as well as depression, hysteria, and hypochondria. You may have more frequent nightmares and trouble sleeping for many years if you were exposed to combat. Fifteen percent of Vietnam veterans reported regular nightmares 18 years after combat.[18]

What is post-traumatic stress disorder?

Post-traumatic stress disorder, or PTSD, is a psychiatric disorder that can occur if you experience or witness a traumatic event such as killing or rape. PTSD sufferers often relive the experience through nightmares and flashbacks. They have difficulty sleeping. They feel detached or estranged. These symptoms can significantly impair daily life.[19]

How common is PTSD?

About 7.8 percent of Americans will experience PTSD at some point in their life, with women (10.4 percent) twice as likely to as men (5 percent). Combat exposure is one of the most common causes. Roughly one third of Vietnam theater veterans experienced full PTSD at some point after discharge, and another 22 percent experienced partial PTSD. Roughly half of World War II POWs experienced symptoms of PTSD nearly 40 years after their imprisonment. After the Gulf War, roughly 20 percent of soldiers exhibited some PTSD symptoms within six months of returning home.[20]

Are female soldiers as likely to develop PTSD?

Women in the military develop PTSD at about the same rate as men, but for different reasons. For men, the lead cause of PTSD is combat exposure. In civilian life, sexual assault is the number one cause of PTSD among women. In the military it is no different. Sexual stress causes almost four times more PTSD among military women than does duty-related stress.[21]

Who is most at risk for PTSD in combat?

Among men, Hispanics and blacks are more susceptible than whites. The Army and the Marine Corps are the most susceptible services. In all branches, the lower ranks are more likely to experience PTSD.[22]

What will the effect on my family be if I develop PTSD?

Vietnam veterans with PTSD were twice as likely to get divorced as those without, and three times more likely to go through multiple divorces. About 60 percent of veterans with PTSD report medium-high to high levels of marital problems. Your children will be more likely to have behavioral problems. Family violence is significantly more prevalent when the father has PTSD.[23]

Is it true that you cannot get PTSD if you are also injured?

No. This was once believed to be the case. Receiving a head injury in combat increases your chances of PTSD.[24]

What does PTSD damage?

The front part of the brain. If you develop PTSD, your sense of smell may be weakened. You may have trouble learning new words. You may also hear things. Common auditory hallucinations include hearing voices in your head, especially the imagined voice of someone you have killed.[25]

Could my PTSD be harmful to others?

Yes. You may misidentify someone or something as an enemy. PTSD sufferers have violently attacked people and objects while under the influence of a combat flashback.[26]

Will I remember the event that caused my PTSD?

Probably. Memory becomes unreliable as symptoms of PTSD increase, but strengthens around traumatic events, both real and imagined. You will remember most of the incident that caused your trauma, but you will also "remember" other traumatic events that did not occur.[27]

Can PTSD be cured?

No, but treatments can minimize outbreaks. The most successful are medication and cognitive-behavioral therapy—talking through the trauma and processing it slowly. Sertraline (Zoloft) and paroxetine (Paxil) are approved for treating PTSD. Some success has also been reported with eye movement desensitization and reprocessing. Mildly to moderately affected PTSD patients are helped by group therapy.[28]

Will war make me sick?

Perhaps. Deployed personnel are typically exposed to substances that have not been fully tested. The chronic fatigue, stress, and trauma of war may make you more susceptible to long-term illness.

Some Vietnam veterans say that the herbicide Agent Orange, sprayed by the military to clear the jungle of foliage, gave them cancer and caused birth defects among their children. Studies on the topic are inconclusive. The studies have shown that veterans and their children do not have an elevated risk of birth defects. Their cancer rates are similar to that of the general population. Thousands of veterans of the Gulf War reported "Gulf War syndrome." The symptoms include muscle and joint pain, rectal bleeding, respiratory problems, fatigue, headaches, nausea, sleep disorders, weight and memory loss, rashes, fevers, impotence, miscarriage, and birth defects. Gulf War veterans blame burning oil wells, depleted uranium, chemical warfare, infectious diseases, and drugs and vaccinations dispensed by the military for the syndrome.[29]

Will I be more likely to commit suicide if I am in a war?

Only slightly. Studies of Vietnam War, Korean War, and World War II veterans report a five-year postwar window of slightly increased mortality for veterans—perhaps 25 percent higher than average. This includes all forms of death, not only suicide. Vietnam veterans, five years after their service, have a suicide rate similar to that of the general population.[30]

Will I be more likely to be homeless?

No. Although one third of America's homeless are veterans, 250,000 of them on any given day, studies indicate that neither military service nor exposure to combat are related to an increased risk of homelessness.[31]

Will I receive any compensation if I am permanently disabled in war?

Yes. The military offers disability compensation. If you are permanently disabled by your military service you will receive a monthly benefit payment. The payment will vary based on the degree of your disability. If you are 10 percent disabled, you will receive $104 per month. If you are 100 percent disabled, you will receive $2,193 per month. The benefits are free from state and federal tax.[32]

Does winning a Medal of Honor have any effect on civilian life?

Veterans who have been awarded a Medal of Honor are entitled to $600 per month for life, a right to burial at Arlington National Cemetery, admission for them or their children to a service academy (if they qualify and quotas permit), and free travel on government aircraft to almost anywhere in the world, on a space-available basis. In March 2003, there were 138 living Medal of Honor recipients.[33]

Will my war get a memorial in Washington, D.C.?

Not necessarily—there is no monument for the Gulf War. If your war does get a memorial, it will be because of a private effort. A World War II memorial will be completed in Washington in 2004. It will be the result of $174 million in private pledges, $16 million from the federal government, a national design competition, and years of planning and lobbying. Legislation authorizing the monument was first introduced in 1987.[34]

How will I feel when I hear war discussed?

It may trigger a flashback. You will be more likely to recall the stress of battle in conversations about war with non-family members than with family members. You are more likely to have a flashback triggered by a TV show or movie than by a conversation, and slightly less likely to have one triggered by a dream or nightmare.[35]

What will I miss most about combat?

The camaraderie. Going through combat together produces a feeling of solidarity that is almost impossible to replicate.[36]

Will I stay in touch with my comrades?

Probably not. Comradeship is based on shared danger, a common goal, and close proximity. It is often mistaken for friendship, but is in fact the very opposite. J. Glenn Gray writes that the essential difference between friendship and comradeship is that friendship creates "a heightened awareness of the self," while comradeship is predicated on "the suppression of self-awareness." He also notes that "suffering and danger cannot create friendship, but they make all the difference in comradeship. Men who have lived through hard and dangerous experiences together are frequently deceived about their relationship. Comrades love one another like brothers, and under the influence of shared experience commonly vow to remain true friends for the rest of their lives. But when other experiences intervene and common memories dim, they gradually become strangers."[37]

Can I wear my medals on my civilian clothes?

You can wear your medals on your civilian clothes at occasions of a military character.[38]

Do I get to keep my uniform?

Yes. You are allowed to wear it, or the contemporary uniform for your rank, at occasions of a military character, provided your grooming meets military standards: no beards or long hair on men. When disposing of an old uniform, you are to make sure no nonveteran acquires it.[39]

NOTES

CHAPTER ONE

1. Daniel Smith, "The World at War: January 2003," *Defense Monitor* (Washington, D.C.: Center for Defense Information, 2003), 1–8.

2. R. Paul Shaw and Yuwa Wang, *Genetic Seeds of Warfare: Evolution, Nationalism, and Patriotism* (Boston: Unwin Hyman, 1989), 3.

3. Douglas Holdstock, "Morbidity and Mortality among Soldiers and Civilians," in *War or Health? A Reader*, eds. Ilkka Taipale et al. (New York: Zed Books, 2002), 183–97; Anna Sillanpaa, "The Effect of War on Population," in *War or Health? A Reader*, eds. Ilkka Taipale et al. (New York: Zed Books, 2002), 203.

4. U.S. Department of State, "Military Expenditures and Arms Transfers 1999–2000" (Washington, D.C.: March 2003), www.state.gov/documents/organization/18725.pdf.

5. Daniel Smith, "The World at War."

6. Laura Kauppinen, "Psychological Theories of Aggressive Behavior," in *War or Health? A Reader*, 355–65.

7. Joshua S. Goldstein, *War and Gender: How Gender Shapes the War System and Vice Versa* (Cambridge: Cambridge University Press, 2001), 10; Military Family Resource Center, "2001 Demographics: Profile of the Military Community" (Arlington, Va.: 2002).

8. U.S. Army Center of Military History, "Full-Text Listings of Medal of Honor Citations" (Washington, D.C.: 2002), www.army.mil/cmh-pg/moh1.htm; David S. Pierson, "Natural Killers: Turning the Tide of Battle," *Military Review*, May 1999.

9. U.S. Army Field Manual 22-51, "Leaders' Manual for Combat Stress Control" (Washington, D.C.: 29 December 1994), 3-3.

10. Eric V. Larson, "Casualties and Consensus: The Historical Role of Casualties in Domestic Support for U.S. Military Operations" (MR-726-OSD, Santa Monica, Calif.: RAND, 1996).

11. U.S. Department of Defense, "Active Duty Military Personnel by Rank/Grade" (Washington, D.C.: 31 January 2003), web1.whs.osd.mil/mmid/military/ms11.pdf; U.S. Department of Defense, "Defense Almanac" (Washington, D.C.: 2003), www.defenselink.mil/pubs/almanac.

12. U.S. Department of Veterans Affairs, "America's Wars Fact Sheet" (Washington, D.C.: May 2001), www.va.gov/pressrel/amwars01.htm.

13. U.S. Department of Defense, "Military Casualty Information" (Washington, D.C.), web1.whs.osd.mil; Douglas Holdstock, "Morbidity and Mortality," 183–97; Carter Malkasian, *The Korean War: 1950–1953* (Chicago, Ill.: Fitzroy Dearborn, 2001), 88; Thomas C. Thayer, *War Without Fronts: The American Experience in Vietnam* (Boulder: Westview Press, 1985), 104, 126–9.

14. Center for Strategic and Budgetary Assessments, "Federal Spending and the Gross Domestic Product" (Washington, D.C.: February 2002); U.S. Office of Management and Budget, "Budget of the United States Government, Fiscal Year 2004" (Washington, D.C.); Seymour Melman, *After Capitalism: From Managerialism to Workplace Democracy* (New York: Alfred A. Knopf, 2001); U.S. Department of Defense, "National Defense Budget Estimates for FY2003" (Washington, D.C.: 2002), tables 7-6 and 7-7, www.defensedaily.com/budgets/fy03_greenbook.pdf.

15. William Nordhaus, "The Economic Consequences of a War with Iraq," in *War with Iraq: Costs, Consequences, and Alternatives* (Cambridge, Mass.: American Academy of Arts and Sciences, 2002), 57–95.

16. U.S. Department of Defense, "DoD Top 100 Companies and Their Subsidiaries, Fiscal Year 2002" (Washington, D.C.), www.dior.whs.mil; U.S. Department of Defense, "National Defense Budget Estimates for FY2003," tables 7-6 and 7-7.

17. U.S. Department of Defense, "National Defense Budget Estimates for FY2003," table 7-7.

18. Center for Responsive Politics, "Defense: Long-Term Contribution Trends" (Washington, D.C.: 2003).

19. Richard F. Grimmett, "Conventional Arms Transfer to Developing Nations, 1994–2001" (Washington, D.C.: Congressional Research Service, 6 August 2002), fpc.state.gov/documents/organization/12632.pdf.

20. Federation of American Scientists, Arms Sales Monitoring Project, "2002 Notifications to Congress of Pending U.S. Arms Transfers" (Washington, D.C.).

21. Richard F. Grimmett, "Conventional Arms Transfer."

22. Barry S. Levy and Victor W. Sidel, "The Health and Social Consequences of Diversion of Economic Resources to War and Preparation for War," in *War or Health? A Reader*, 208–21; Victoria Garcia, "A Risky Business: U.S. Arms Exports to Countries Where Terror Thrives" (Washington, D.C.: Center for Defense Information, 29 November 2001); William D. Hartung and Frida Berrigan, "U.S. Arms Transfers and Security Assistance to Israel" (New York: Arms Trade Resource Center, World Policy Institute, 6 May 2002).

23. Carter Malkasian, *The Korean War*, 88; Douglas Holdstock, "Morbidity and Mortality," 183–97; Thomas C. Thayer, *War Without Fronts*, 126–9; William Eckhardt, "Wars and War-Related Deaths, 1500–1990," in *World Military and Social Expenditures 1991*, by Ruth Leger Sivard (Washington, D.C.: World Priorities, 1991), 22–5.

24. Eric Carlton, *Massacres: An Historical Perspective* (Brookfield, Vt.: Ashgate Publishing Company, 1994), 142–3; David M. Glantz, *The Battle for Leningrad, 1941–1944* (Lawrence, Kans.: University of Kansas Press, 2002), 468; James Lyons, "Heat in Gulf to Rocket," London *Daily Mirror*, 2 April 2003.

25. United Nations High Commissioner for Refugees, "The State of the World's Refugees. 50 Years of Humanitarian Action" (Geneva: 2002), 219, 246; Graca Machel, *The Impact of War on Children* (London: Hurst & Company, 2001), 26; United Nations High Commissioner for Refugees, "Refugees Flee in All Directions as Conflict Spreads in Eastern Liberia," www.unhcr.ch, 3 April 2003.

26. Michael J. Toole, "Displaced Persons and War," in *War and Public Health*, eds. Barry S. Levy and Victor W. Sidel (Washington, D.C.: American Public Health Association, 2000), 202–3.

27. Graca Machel, *The Impact of War on Children*, 1–6.

28. Graca Machel, *The Impact of War on Children*, 7, 14; Vappu Taipale, "Children and War," in *War or Health? A Reader*, 249–58.

29. Graca Machel, *The Impact of War on Children*, 8–12.

30. Mary Elizabeth Ashford and Yolanda Huet-Vaughn, "The Impact of War on Women," in *War and Public Health*, eds. Barry S. Levy and Victor W. Sidel (Washington, D.C.: American Public Health Association, 2000), 186–9.

31. United Nations General Assembly, "Convention on the Prevention and Punishment of the Crime of Genocide" (1948), art. II; Alexander Laban Hinton ed., *Annihilating Difference: The Anthropology of Genocide* (Berkeley: University of California Press, 2002).

32. Craig Etcheson, *The Rise and Demise of Democratic Kampuchea* (Boulder: Westview Press, 1984); Kenneth J. Campbell, *Genocide and the Global Village* (New York: Palgrave, 2001); Alexandre Kimenyi and Otis L. Scott, eds., *Anatomy of Genocide: State-Sponsored Mass-Killings in the Twentieth Century* (Lewiston, NY: Edwin Mellen Press, 2001), 422–4; Alex Alvarez, *Governments, Citizens, and Genocide: A Comparative and Interdisciplinary Approach* (Bloomington: Indiana University Press, 2001), 12; Human Rights Watch, "The Anfal Campaign Against the Kurds: A Middle East Watch Report" (New York: 1993).

CHAPTER TWO

1. U.S. Department of Defense, "Defense Almanac" (Washington, D.C.: 2003), www.defenselink.mil/pubs/almanac; U.S. Army, www.army.mil, 14 April 2003; U.S. Navy, www.navy.mil, 14 April 2003; U.S. Air Force, www.af.mil, 14 April 2003; U.S Marine Corps, www.usmc.mil, 14 April 2003; U.S. Coast Guard, www.uscg.mil, 14 April 2003; Robert Komer, "Strategymaking in the Pentagon," in *Reorganizing America's Defense: Leadership in War and Peace*, eds. Robert J. Art, Vincent Davis, and Samuel P. Huntington (Washington, D.C.: Pergamon-Brassey's International Defense Publishers, 1985), 207–19.

2. U.S. Department of Defense, "Defense Almanac"; U.S. Department of Defense, the Joint Chiefs of Staff, www.dtic.mil/jcs, 14 April 2003.

3. Michael J. Wilson, James B. Greenlees, Tracey Hagerty, D. Wayne Hintze, and Jerome D. Lehnus, "Youth Attitude Tracking Study 1998: Propensity and Advertising Report" (Rockville, Md.: Westat, Inc. & Arlington, Va.: Defense Manpower Data Center, 17 January 2000), table 4.1.

4. U.S. Army Recruiting Command, "FY 2002 Demo Profile" (Fort Know, Ky.: 2002).

5. Dave Grossman, *On Killing: The Psychological Cost of Learning to Kill in War and Society* (Boston: Little, Brown and Company, 1995), 142–55; U.S. Army TRADOC Regulation 350-1, "Army Training" (Ft. Monroe, Va.: 1 August 1983), sec. 1-1.

6. Anthony Kellett, *Combat Motivation: The Behavior of Soldiers in Battle* (Boston: Kluwer, 1982), 73–4; Lawrence B. Radine, *The Taming of the Troops: Social Control in the United States Army* (Westport, Conn.: Greenwood Press, 1977), 40–3; U.S. Army TRADOC Regulation 350-6, "Enlisted Initial Entry Training (IET) Policies and Administration" (Ft. Monroe, Va.: 3 July 2001).

7. Rose M. Popovich, John W. Gardner, Robert Potter, Joseph J. Knapik, and Bruce H. Jones, "Effect of Rest from Running on Overuse Injuries in Army Basic Training," *American Journal of Preventive Medicine* 18.3, Supplement 1 (April 2000), 147–55.

8. U.S. Army Field Manual 21-20, "Physical Fitness Training" (Washington, D.C.: 30 September 1992), fig. 11-1.

9. U.S. Army TRADOC Regulation 350-6, sec. 2-6; Lawrence B. Radine, *The Taming of the Troops*, 39–43.

10. Gerry J. Gilmore, "Recruit Attrition Rates Fall Across the Services" (Alexandria, Va.: Armed Forces Information Service, 13 August 2001).

11. Gerry J. Gilmore, "Recruit Attrition Rates Fall."

12. Dave Grossman, *On Killing*, 250–6.

13. James H. Toner, *Morals Under the Gun: The Cardinal Virtues, Military Ethics, and American Society* (Lexington: University Press of Kentucky, 2000).

14. U.S. Department of Defense Directive 1304.26, "Qualification Standards for Enlistment, Appointment, and Induction" (Washington, D.C.: 21 December 1993).

15. U.S. Army Regulation 40-501, "Standards of Medical Fitness" (Washington, D.C.: 30 September 2002).

16. Lawrence M. Baskir and William A. Strauss, *Chance and Circumstance* (New York: Alfred A. Knopf, 1978), 5, 22–61; Sherry Gershon Gottlieb, *Hell No, We Won't Go! Resisting the Draft During the Vietnam War* (New York: Penguin, 1991).

17. Christian Bauman, interview by author, New York, 4 April 2003.

18. John Ellis, *The Sharp End: The Fighting Man in World War II* (London: Pimlico, 1993), 158.

19. U.S. Army John F. Kennedy Special Warfare Center and School, "Special Forces Pipeline" (Key West, Fla.), www.soc.mil/swcs/museum/pipeline.shtml, 9 April 2003; U.S. Navy Special Warfare, www.sealchallenge.navy.mil, 14 April 2003.

20. Peter Watson, *War on the Mind: The Military Uses and Abuses of Psychology* (New York: Basic Books, 1978), 371.

21. U.S. Army John F. Kennedy Special Warfare Center and School, "Special Forces Pipeline"; Carl Stiner, Tony Koltz, and Tom Clancy, *Shadow Warriors: Inside the U.S. Army Special Forces* (New York: Putnam, 2002), 153; Anna Simons, *The Company They Keep: Life Inside the U.S. Army Special Forces* (New York: Free Press, 1997), 60; Dave Grossman, *On Killing*, 67–9.

22. U.S. Department of Defense, "The Ninth Quadrennial Review of Military Compensation, 2001" (Washington, D.C.), vol. II, ch. 1; U.S. Defense Finance and

Accounting Service, "Complete Active Duty and Reserve Monthly Drill Pay Tables, 2001" (Washington, D.C.).

23. Rudi Williams, "Chu Says Benefits Are Good, but Improvements Can Be Made" (Alexandria, Va.: Armed Forces Information Service, 24 May 2002).

24. Beth Asch, James R. Hosek, Jeremy Arkes, C. Christine Fair, Jennifer Sharp, and Mark Totten, *Military Recruiting and Retention After the Fiscal Year 2000 Military Pay Legislation* (MR-1532-OSD, Santa Monica, Calif.: RAND, 2002), table A.1; Defense Manpower Data Center, "2002 Active Duty Status of Forces Survey: Overview Briefing" (Arlington, Va.: 31 January 2003), 64–5; David M. Halbfinger and Steven A. Holmes, "Military Mirrors a Working-Class America," *New York Times*, 30 March 2003, A1.

25. Beth Asch et al., *Military Recruiting*, ch. 4.

26. U.S. Department of Defense Directive 1327.5, "Leave and Liberty" (Washington, D.C.: 10 September 1997), 5.5, 6.2.1; U.S. Air Force AFI 36-3003, "Military Leave Program" (Washington, D.C.: 14 April 2000), 4.11.3.

27. U.S. Office of the Under Secretary of Defense for Personnel and Readiness, "Military Compensation" (Washington, D.C.: 2003), dod.mil/militarypay, 1 April 2003.

28. U.S. Department of Defense, "Defense Science Board Task Force on Quality of Life" (Washington, D.C.: October 1995), 3; Richard J. Buddin, Carole Roan Gresenz, Susan D. Hosek, Marc N. Elliott, and Jennifer Hawes-Dawson, *An Evaluation of Housing Options for Military Families* (MR-1020-OSD, Santa Monica, Calif: RAND, 1999), ch. 1; Defense Technical Information Center, "Basic Allowance for Housing" (Fort Belvoir, Va.: 2000).

29. U.S. Department of Defense Instruction 1404.12, "Employment of Spouses of Active Duty Military Members Stationed Worldwide" (Washington, D.C.: 12 January 1989), 2.2, 4.3.1.

30. James Hosek, Beth Asch, C. Christine Fair, Craig Martin, and Michael Mattock, *Married to the Military: The Employment and Earnings of Military Wives Compared with Those of Civilian Wives* (MR-1565 OSD, Santa Monica, Calif: RAND, 2002), xi–xvi.

31. U.S. General Accounting Office, "Military Personnel: Longer Time Between Moves Related to Higher Satisfaction and Retention" (Washington, D.C.: August 2001), 1–2, 10, 12.

32. U.S. General Accounting Office, "Military Personnel," 15, 20.

33. U.S. General Accounting Office, "Military Personnel," 24–9.

34. Michelle L. Kelley, "The Effects of Deployment on Traditional and Nontraditional Military Families: Navy Mothers and Their Children," in *Military Brats and Other Global Nomads: Growing Up in Organization Families*, ed. Morten G. Ender (Westport, Conn.: Praeger, 2002), 3–7; Karen Cachevki Williams and LisaMarie Mariglia, "Military Brats: Issues and Associations in Adulthood," in *Military Brats and Other Global Nomads: Growing Up in Organization Families*, ed. Morten G. Ender (Westport, Conn.: Praeger, 2002), 68; Edna J. Hunter-King, "Long-Term Effects on Children of a Parent Missing in Wartime," in *The Military Family in Peace and War*, ed. Florence W. Kaslow (New York: Springer Publishing Company, 1993), pp. 48–65.

35. William Ruger, Sven E. Wilson, and Shawn L. Waddoups, "Warfare and Welfare: Military Service, Combat, and Marital Dissolution," *Armed Forces & Society* 29.1 (Fall 2002), 99; Military Family Resource Center, "2001 Demographics: Profile of the Military Community" (Arlington, Va.: 2002), ii–v; National Center for Health Statistics, "Births, Marriages, Divorces, and Deaths: Provisional Data for January–December 2000," *National Vital Statistics Reports* 49.6 (22 August 2001), table 12.

36. Mary Elizabeth Ashford and Yolanda Huet-Vaughn, "The Impact of War on Women," in *War and Public Health*, eds. Barry S. Levy and Victor W. Sidel (Washington, D.C.: American Public Health Association, 2000), 192.

37. U.S. Office of the Assistant Secretary of Defense (Force Management Policy), "Population Representation in the Military Services: Fiscal Year 1999" (Washington, D.C.: November 2000), secs. 7-5–7-7.

38. Military Family Resource Center, "2001 Demographics Report," secs. 2-13–2-14; U.S. Census Bureau, "Census 2000" (Washington, D.C.), table 2-1; David M. Halbfinger and Steven A. Holmes, "Military Mirrors a Working-Class America"; Diego Ibarguen, "Bush Sees 2 Marines Wounded in Iraq Become U.S. Citizens," *Philadelphia Inquirer*, 11 April 2003.

39. Charles C. Moskos and John Sibley Butler, *All That We Can Be: Black Leadership and Racial Integration the Army Way* (New York: Basic Books, 1996), 5, 40–1, 66–7.

40. Charles C. Moskos and John Sibley Butler, *All That We Can Be*, 38; Aline O. Quester and Curtis L. Gilroy, "America's Military: A Coat of Many Colors" (Alexandria, Va.: Center for Naval Analysis, July 2001), 27–28; Margaret Harrell et al., *Barriers to Minority Participation in Special Operations Forces* (MR-1042-SOCOM, Santa Monica, Calif.: RAND, 1999), 48–9.

41. Aline O. Quester and Curtis L. Gilroy, "America's Military," 27–28; David M. Halbfinger and Steven A. Holmes, "Military Mirrors a Working-Class America"; Margaret Harrell et al., *Barriers to Minority Participation*, xiv–xv, 48–9.

42. Margaret C. Harrell and Laura L. Miller, *New Opportunities for Military Women: Effects Upon Readiness, Cohesion, and Morale* (MR-896-OSD, Santa Monica, Calif.: RAND, 1997), 13–15, 20, 22; Jason B. Baker, "A Jump to Celebrate," *Soldiers* 57:6 (June 2002), 27; Jay Parker, interview, West Point, N.Y., 22 April 2003; U.S. General Accounting Office, "Gender Issues: Information on DOD's Assignment Policy and Direct Ground Combat Definition" (Washington, D.C.: October 1998), GAO-NSIAD-99-7, 1–25.

43. Joshua S. Goldstein, *War and Gender: How Gender Shapes the War System and Vice Versa* (Cambridge: Cambridge University Press, 2001), 139, 337.

44. Military Family Resource Center, "2001 Demographics Report," ii, sec. 2.34.

45. Dana Priest, "Pregnancy Often Causes Tension in Army's Ranks," *Washington Post*, 30 December 1997, A6.

46. Dana Priest, "Pregnancy Often Causes Tension," A6; Lyndsey Layton, "Navy Women Finding Ways to Adapt to a Man's World," *Washington Post*, 15 March 2003, A15.

Notes

47. Charles Moskos, "Army Women," *Atlantic Monthly* 266.2 (August 1990), 71–8.

48. Margaret C. Harrell and Laura L. Miller, *New Opportunities for Military Women*, 77–81; Susan D. Hosek et al., *Minority and Gender Differences in Officer Career Progression* (MR-1184-OSD, Santa Monica, Calif.: RAND, 2001), xv–xvii, 76–81.

49. Lisa D. Bastian, Anita R. Lancaster, and Heidi E. Reyst, "Department of Defense 1995 Sexual Harassment Survey" (Arlington, Va.: Defense Manpower Data Center, December 1996), figs. 1, 2, 3, 9, 13.

50. Lisa D. Bastian, Anita R. Lancaster, and Heidi E. Reyst, "Department of Defense 1995 Sexual Harassment Survey," table 6.

51. U.S. Department of Defense Directive 1304.26, "Qualification Standards," E1.2.8.1

52. National Defense Research Institute, *Sexual Orientation and U.S. Military Personnel Policy: Options and Assessment* (MR-323-OSD, Santa Monica, Calif.: RAND, 1993), 49; Randy Shilts, *Conduct Unbecoming: Lesbians and Gays in the U.S. Military* (New York: St. Martin's Press, 1993), 1; Servicemembers Legal Defense Network, "Conduct Unbecoming: The Ninth Annual Report on 'Don't Ask, Don't Tell, Don't Pursue, Don't Harass'" (Washington, D.C.: 2003), 13, 23, 27, 33.

53. National Defense Research Institute, *Sexual Orientation and U.S. Military Personnel*, 217.

54. National Defense Research Institute, *Sexual Orientation and U.S. Military Personnel*, 217.

55. David McCormick, *The Downsized Warrior: America's Army in Transition* (New York: New York University Press, 1998), 3, 112–6, 123; David H. Marlowe, *Psychological and Psychosocial Consequences of Combat and Deployment with Special Emphasis on the Gulf War* (MR-1018/11-OSD, Santa Monica, Calif.: RAND, 22 January 2001), 155.

56. Roger Little, "Friendships in the Military Community," in *Research in the Interweave of Social Roles: Friendship* vol. 2 (Greenwich, Conn.: Jai Press, 1981), 221–35.

57. David McCormick, *The Downsized Warrior*; Stephen L. Mangum and David E. Ball, "Military Skill Training: Some Evidence of Transferability," *Armed Forces and Society* 13.3 (Spring 1987), 425–41; Antonina Dashkina, "The System of Social Support and Help to Ex-Officers and Their Families in Great Britain, the United States of America and Russia" (Brussels: NATO Academic Forum Fellowship, 1996).

58. Paul Richard Higate, "Theorizing Continuity: From Military to Civilian Life," *Armed Forces and Society* 27.3 (Spring 2001), 443–60.

59. Rex A. Frank, "Military Retirement in the Post–Cold War Era," in *The Military Family in Peace and War*, ed. Florence W. Kaslow (New York: Springer Publishing Company, 1993), 214–40.

60. Roger Little, "Friendships in the Military Community," 221–35.

CHAPTER THREE

1. David H. Marlowe, *Psychological and Psychosocial Consequences of Combat and Deployment with Special Emphasis on the Gulf War* (MR-1018/11-OSD, Santa Monica, Calif.: RAND, 22 January 2001), 115–43.

2. U.S. Defense Finance and Accounting Service, "Basic Pay—Effective January 1, 2003" (Washington, D.C.).

3. Bernadette M. Marriott, ed., *Food Components to Enhance Performance, Committee on Military Nutrition Research* (Washington, D.C.: Food and Nutrition Board, 1994), 333, 488–9.

4. Center for Army Lessons Learned Handbook 02-8, "Operation Enduring Freedom: Tactics, Techniques, and Procedures" (Ft. Leavenworth, Kans: 2002), ch. 2.

5. Center for Army Lessons Learned Handbook 02-8, ch. 2.

6. Center for Army Lessons Learned Handbook 02-8, ch. 2.

7. Center for Army Lessons Learned Handbook 02-8, ch. 2; *Disaster Preparedness Handbook* (Loudon, NH: Turning Point Communications), www.disastermagazine.com, 11 April 2003, ch 3–2.

8. Center for Army Lessons Learned Handbook 02-8, ch. 2.

9. Center for Army Lessons Learned Handbook 02-8, ch. 2.

10. Michael John Hughey, "The Health Care of Women in Military Settings," *Operational Obstetrics & Gynecology*, 2d ed. (NAVMEDPUB 6300-2D, 1 January 2000), www.vnh.org, 4 April 2003.

11. Center for Army Lessons Learned Handbook 02-8, ch. 2.

12. Michael John Hughey, "The Health Care of Women."

13. David H. Marlowe, *Psychological and Psychosocial Consequences*, 115–43.

14. U.S. Army Field Manual 22-51, "Leaders' Manual for Combat Stress Control" (Washington, D.C.: 29 September 1994), sec. A-9.

15. David H. Marlowe, *Psychological and Psychosocial Consequences*, 115–43.

16. Thomas M. Huber, "Deception: Deceiving the Enemy in Operation Desert Storm," in *Combined Arms Battle Since 1939*, ed. Roger J. Spiller (Ft. Leavenworth, Kans.: U.S. Army Command and General Staff College Press, 1992), 59–65.

17. U.S. Army Field Manual 22-51, A-6; U.S. Department of Defense 4525.6-M, "Department of Defense Postal Manual" (Washington, D.C.: 15 August 2002), C2.8.

18. U.S. Army Family Liaison Office, "Frequently Asked Questions," www.aflo.org, 4 April 2003.

19. Simon H. Pincus et al., "The Emotional Cycle of Deployment: A Military Family Perspective," *U.S. Army Medical Department Journal*, April–June 2001.

20. Roger W. Little, "Buddy Relations and Combat Performance," in *The New Military: Changing Patterns of Organization*, ed. Morris Janowitz (New York: Russell Sage Foundation, 1964), 195–223.

21. David H. Marlowe, *Psychological and Psychosocial Consequences*, 115–43.

22. U.S. Army Field Manual 22-51, ch. 3.

23. Don Vaughan, "Relying on Luck," *The Retired Officer Magazine*, November 2002.

24. Joshua S. Goldstein, *War and Gender: How Gender Shapes the War System and Vice Versa* (Cambridge: Cambridge University Press, 2001), 337.

25. Michael J. Davidson, *A Guide to Military Criminal Law* (Annapolis, Md.: Naval Institute Press, 1999), 82–95.

26. David H. Marlowe, *Psychological and Psychosocial Consequences*, table 10.3.

27. Joshua S. Goldstein, *War and Gender*, 348.

28. David H. Marlowe, *Psychological and Psychosocial Consequences*, 145–58.

29. U.S. Central Command, "Prohibited Activities for U.S. Department of Defense Personnel Serving in the United States Central Command," www.centcom.mil, 4 April 2003.

30. Joint Service Committee on Military Justice, "Manual for Courts-Martial, United States, 2000 Edition" (Washington, D.C.: 2000), IV-54–58.

31. Clifton D. Bryant, *Khaki-Collar Crime: Deviant Behavior in the Military Context* (New York: Free Press, 1979), 174, P. Gunby, "Service in Strict Islamic Nation Removes Alcohol, Other Drugs from Major Problem List," *Journal of the American Medical Association* 265 (1991), 560–62.

32. Robert M. Bray, "1998 Department of Defense Survey of Health Related Behaviors Among Military Personnel" (Research Triangle Park, N.C.: Research Triangle Institute, 1999).

33. B.H.A. Jones and B.C. Hansen, eds., *Injuries in the Military: A Hidden Epidemic* (Aberdeen Proving Ground, MD: U.S. Army Center for Health Promotion and Preventive Medicine, November 1996), table 5-4.

34. U.S. Department of Defense Information Paper: "Vaccine Use During the Gulf War" (Washington, D.C.: 7 December 2000), www.gulflink.osd.mil/va, 4 April 2003.

35. Jill R. Keeler, "Pyridostigmine Used as a Nerve Agent Pretreatment Under Wartime Conditions," *Journal of the American Medical Association* 286.5 (7 August 1991), 694–5; David H. Marlowe, *Psychological and Psychosocial Consequences*, 140–1.

36. Center for Army Lessons Learned Handbook 02-8, ch. 2; James E. Fitzpatrick, "Superficial Fungal Skin Diseases," in *Military Dermatology, Part III: Disease and the Environment*, eds. William D. James and Russ Zajtchuck (Falls Church, Va.: Office of the Army Surgeon General, 1994), 425.

37. Center for Army Lessons Learned Handbook 02-8, ch. 2; Kenneth C. Hyams et al., "The Impact of Infectious Diseases on the Health of U.S. Troops Deployed to the Persian Gulf During Operations Desert Shield/Desert Storm," *Clinical Infectious Diseases* 20 (1995), 1497–504.

38. U.S. Army STP 21-1-SMCT, "Soldier's Manual of Common Tasks, Skill Level 1" (Washington, D.C.: 1 October 1990).

39. U.S. Army Field Manual 22-51, A-9.

40. David H. Marlowe, *Psychological and Psychosocial Consequences*, 115–43.

41. Center for Army Lessons Learned Handbook 96-3, "Own the Night! Small Unit Night Fighter Manual" (Ft. Leavenworth, Kans.: 1997), ch. 1.

42. Neil Creighton, Alpha Tank, Task Force 3-15 Infantry, in Alex Vernon, *The Eyes of Orion: Five Tank Lieutenants in the Persian Gulf War* (Kent, Ohio: Kent State University Press, 1999).

43. U.S. Army Field Manual 6-22.5, "Combat Stress" (Washington, D.C.: 23 June 2000), 59, 62, 74.

44. Center for Army Lessons Learned Handbook 02-8, ch. 2.

45. Center for Army Lessons Learned Handbook 02-8, ch. 2.

46. Center for Army Lessons Learned Handbook 02-8, ch. 2.

47. Charles C. Moskos, *The American Enlisted Man: The Rank and File in Today's Military* (New York: Russell Sage Foundation, 1970).

48. John Ellis, *The Sharp End: The Fighting Man in World War II* (London: Pimlico, 1993); U.S. Department of Defense, "Military Casualty Information" (Washington, D.C.: 15 March 2003), web1.whs.osd.mil/mmid/casualty/castop.htm, 19 April 2003; Dave Grossman and Bruce K. Siddle, "Psychological Effects of Combat," in *Encyclopedia of Violence, Peace, and Conflict* (San Diego: Academic Press, 1999).

CHAPTER FOUR

1. Ronald F. Bellamy and Russ Zajtchuk, "The Physics and Biophysics of Wound Ballistics," in *Conventional Warfare: Ballistic, Blast, and Burn Injuries*, eds. Ronald F. Bellamy and Russ Zajtchuk (Falls Church, Va.: Office of the Army Surgeon General, 1989), 108–19.

2. Vincent J.M. Di Maio, *Gunshot Wounds: Practical Aspects of Firearms, Ballistics, and Forensic Techniques* (New York: Elsevier, 1985), 144–55.

3. George Orwell, "The Spanish Civil War: Wounded by a Fascist Sniper, near Huesca, 20 May 1937," in *Eyewitness to History*, ed. John Carey (Cambridge, Mass.: Harvard University Press, 1988), 521–22.

4. Hans Husum, *War Surgery Field Manual* (Penang, Malaysia: Third World Network, 1995), 124.

5. Matti Ponteva, "Military Medicine" in *War or Health? A Reader*, eds. Ilkka Taipale et al. (New York: Zed Books, 2002), 60; Michael Carey et al., "Ballistic Helmets and Aspects of Their Design," *Neurosurgery* 47 (2000), 678–89.

6. Ronald F. Bellamy and Russ Zajtchuk, "Assessing the Effectiveness of Conventional Weapons," in *Conventional Warfare: Ballistic, Blast, and Burn Injuries*, eds. Ronald F. Bellamy and Russ Zajtchuk (Falls Church, Va.: Office of the Army Surgeon General, 1989), 53–80.

7. Ronald F. Bellamy and Russ Zajtchuk, "Assessing the Effectiveness of Conventional Weapons," 53–80.

8. Ronald F. Bellamy and Russ Zajtchuk, "Assessing the Effectiveness of Conventional Weapons," 53–80.

9. William G. Cioffi, Jr. et al, "The Management of Burn Injury," in *Conventional Warfare: Ballistic, Blast, and Burn Injuries*, eds. Ronald F. Bellamy and Russ Zajtchuk (Falls Church, Va.: Office of the Army Surgeon General, 1989), 350.

10. O.N. Gofrit et al., "Accurate Anatomical Location of War Injuries: Analysis of the Lebanon War Fatal Casualties and the Proposition of New Principles for

the Design of Military Personal Armour System," *Injury* 27.8 (October 1996), 577–81; Jean-Claude Sarron et al., "Consequences of Nonpenetrating Projectile Impact on a Protected Head: Study of Rear Effects of Protections," *The Journal of Trauma: Injury, Infection, and Critical Care* 49.5 (November 2000), 923–29; Robert L. Mabry et al., "United States Army Rangers in Somalia: An Analysis of Combat Casualties on an Urban Battlefield," *The Journal of Trauma: Injury, Infection, and Critical Care* 49.3 (2000), 515–29.

11. Hans Husum, *War Surgery*, 108–9.

12. Ronald F. Bellamy and Russ Zajtchuk, "The Physics and Biophysics of Wound Ballistics," 107–59; Robert L. Mabry et al., "United States Army Rangers," 515–29.

13. Michael J. Davidson, *A Guide to Military Criminal Law* (Annapolis, Md.: Naval Institute Press, 1999), 141; Hans Husum, *War Surgery*, 80.

14. Michael Carey et al., "Ballistic Helmets," 678–89; Michael Carey, "Analysis of Wounds Incurred by U.S. Army Seventh Corps Personnel Treated in Corps Hospitals During Operation Desert Storm, February 20 to March 10, 1991," *Journal of Trauma: Injury, Infection, and Critical Care* 40.3 (1996), S165–8; Robert L. Mabry et al., "United States Army Rangers," 515–29.

15. Robert L. Mabry et al., "United States Army Rangers," 515–29; Manoj Monga et al., "Gunshot Wounds to the Male Genitalia," *The Journal of Trauma: Injury, Infection, and Critical Care* 38.6 (1995), 855–8; Ahmet Fuat Peker et al., "Penile Reconstruction with Prosthesis and Free Skin Graft in a Patient with Land Mine Blast Injury," *The Journal of Urology* 167 (2002), 2133–4.

16. Ronald F. Bellamy and Russ Zajtchuk, "The Weapons of Conventional Land Warfare," in *Conventional Warfare: Ballistic, Blast, and Burn Injuries*, eds. Ronald F. Bellamy and Russ Zajtchuk (Falls Church, Va.: Office of the Army Surgeon General, 1989), 15–37; Dana C. Covey et al., "Field Hospital Treatment of Blast Wounds of the Musculoskeletal System During the Yugoslav Civil War," *Journal of Orthopaedic Trauma* 14.4 (2000), 278–86.; U.S. Army Corps of Engineers, "Fact Sheet: Use ordnance safety precautions at the Camp Robinson Formerly Used Defense Site," (Little Rock, Ark.) September 2001, 2.

17. Hans Husum, *War Surgery*, 81–2.

18. Hans Husum, *War Surgery*, 81–2.

19. Hans Husum, *War Surgery*, 84–6.

20. Ronald F. Bellamy and Russ Zajtchuk, "The Weapons of Conventional Land Warfare," 44–7; M. Tahir Khan et al., "Hindfoot Injuries Due to Land Mine Blast Accidents," *Injury* 33 (2002), 167–71.

21. Ibolja Cernak et al., "Blast Injury From Explosive Munitions," *Journal of Trauma: Injury, Infection, and Critical Care* 47.1 (1999), 96–103; Ronald F. Bellamy and Russ Zajtchuk, "Primary Blast Injury and Basic Research: A Brief History," in *Conventional Warfare: Ballistic, Blast, and Burn Injuries*, 221–7; Ronald F. Bellamy and Russ Zajtchuk, "The Weapons of Conventional Land Warfare," 44–6.

22. Hans Husum, *War Surgery*, 84–6.

23. Hans Husum, *War Surgery*, 88.

24. Hans Husum, *War Surgery*, 89.

25. Robert L. Mabry et al., "United States Army Rangers," 515–29; Ronald F. Bellamy and Russ Zajtchuk, "The Weapons of Conventional Land Warfare," 42–4.

26. Eric Prokosch and Ernst Jan Hogendoorn, "Antipersonnel Weapons," in *War or Health? A Reader*, 73–5.

27. Eric Prokosch and Ernst Jan Hogendoorn, "Antipersonnel Weapons," 73–5.

28. Hans Husum, *War Surgery*, 556–63.

29. Hans Husum, *War Surgery*, 564–74.

30. Eric Prokosch and Ernst Jan Hogendoorn, "Antipersonnel Weapons," 74.

31. U.S. Department of Defense, Deployment Health Support Directorate, Depleted Uranium Information Library, deploymentlink.osd.mil/du_library, 4 April 2003; U.S. Army Center for Health Promotion and Preventative Medicine, "Depleted Uranium—Human Exposure and Health Risk Characterization in Support of the Environmental Exposure Report 'Depleted Uranium in the Gulf' of the Office of the Special Assistant to the Secretary of Defense for Gulf War Illnesses, Medical Readiness, and Military Deployment" (September 2000), www.gulflink. osd.mil, 7 April 2003; Marco Durante and Mariagabriella Pugliese, "Estimates of Radiological Risk from Depleted Uranium Weapons In War Scenarios," *Health Physics* 82 (2002), 14–20; Committee to Review the Health Consequences of Service During the Persian Gulf War, *Health Consequences of Service During the Persian Gulf War: Recommendations for Research and Information Systems* (Washington, D.C.: National Academy Press, 1996), 55–6.

32. Douglas Rokke, former head of the Pentagon's Depleted Uranium Project, untitled remarks (Washington, D.C.: The National Vietnam and Gulf War Veterans Coalition 17th Annual Leadership Breakfast, at the U.S. Senate Caucus Room, 10 November 2000).

33. Philip J. Belmont, Jr. et al., "Incidence, Epidemiology, and Occupational Outcomes of Thoracolumbar Fractures Among U.S. Army Aviators," *Journal of Trauma Injury, Infection, and Critical Care* 50.5 (2001), 855–61; Robert L. Mabry et al., "United States Army Rangers," 515–29.

34. Ronald F. Bellamy and Russ Zajtchuk, "Assessing the Effectiveness of Conventional Weapons," 53–82.

35. Hans Husum, *War Surgery*, 53–82.

36. Hans Husum, *War Surgery*, 107–9.

37. Hans Husum, *War Surgery*, 123–7; Joint Publication 4-02.2, "Joint Tactics, Techniques and Procedures for Patient Movement in Joint Operations" (Washington, D.C.: Joint Chiefs of Staff, 30 December 1996), sec. 1-1.

38. Hans Husum, *War Surgery*, 667–8.

39. Mona P. Ternus, "Bosnia and Kosovo: Aeromedical Evacuation in the Initial Stages of Deployment," *Aviation, Space, and Environmental Medicine* 72.4 (April 2001), 357–60; Joint Publication 4-02.2, sec. 1-1.

40. Hans Husum, *War Surgery*, 642–59.

41. Hans Husum, *War Surgery*, 586.

42. Hans Husum, *War Surgery*, 104.

43. Ronald F. Bellamy and Russ Zajtchuk, "Assessing the Effectiveness of Conventional Weapons," 71–3.

44. Ronald F. Bellamy and Russ Zajtchuk, "Assessing the Effectiveness of Conventional Weapons," 71–3.

45. William G. Cioffi, Jr. et al., "The Management of Burn Injury," 349–68; Chrissie Bosworth Bousfield, ed., *Burn Trauma: Management and Nursing Care* (Philadelphia: Whurr Publishers, 2002), xi.

46. Ronald F. Bellamy and Russ Zajtchuk, "The Weapons of Conventional Land Warfare," 10; U.S. Marine Corps, Equipment Factfile, "M-16A2 5.56mm Rifle," www.hqmc.usmc.mil; U.S. Army, Army Fact File, "M-4 Carbine," www.army.mil/fact_files_site, 9 April 2003.

47. Hans Husum, *War Surgery*, 80.

48. Michael Renner, "Small Arms," in *War or Health? A Reader*, 91–4.

49. Hans Husum, *War Surgery*, 77–80.

50. Ronald F. Bellamy and Russ Zajtchuk, "Evolution of Wound Ballistics: A Brief History," in *Conventional Warfare: Ballistic, Blast, and Burn Injuries*, 89–90; Hans Husum, *War Surgery*, 80.

51. Craig S. Bartlett, "Clinical Update: Gunshot Wound Ballistics," *Clinical Orthopaedics and Related Research* 408 (March 2003), 28–57; Hans Husum, *War Surgery*, 80.

52. Michael J. Davidson, *A Guide to Military Criminal Law*, 140–41.

53. Hans Husum, *War Surgery*, 87.

54. Ronald F. Bellamy and Russ Zajtchuk, "Assessing the Effectiveness of Conventional Weapons," 63–73.

CHAPTER FIVE

1. U.S. Army Field Manual 3-100, "Chemical Operations Principles and Fundamentals" (Washington, D.C.: 8 May 1996), sec. 1-1.

2. *Nuclear Weapons: Report of the Secretary-General of the United Nations* (London: Frances Pinter, 1981), 8–9; Edward M. Spiers, *Weapons of Mass Destruction* (New York: St. Martin's Press, 2000), 2–3.

3. U.S. Army Correspondence Course CM2307, "Nuclear Reporting" (Washington, D.C.: 1 June 1997), lesson 3, pt. A.

4. U.S. Army Field Manual 21-75, "Combat Skills of the Soldier" (Washington, D.C.: 3 August 1984), secs. 5-2–5-3.

5. U.S. Army Field Manual 21-75, sec. 5-3; Kenjiro Yokoro and Nanao Kamada, "The Public Health Effects of the Use of Nuclear Weapons," in *War and Public Health*, eds. Barry S. Levy and Victor W. Sidel (New York: Oxford University Press, 1997), 66–73; Federation of American Scientists, "Special Weapons Primer" (Washington, D.C.), www.fas.org/nuke/intro.

6. Franklin D. Jones, "Neuropsychiatric Casualties of Nuclear, Biological, and Chemical Warfare," in *Textbook of Military Medicine*, eds. Franklin D. Jones et al. (Falls Church, Va.: Office of the Army Surgeon General, U.S. Army, 1995), 105.

7. Anna Sillanpaa, "The Effects of War on Population," in *War or Health? A Reader*, eds. Ilkka Taipale et al. (New York: Zed Books, 2002), 205; Kenjiro Yokoro and Nanao Kamada, "The Public Health Effects," 65.

8. U.S. Army Field Manual 21-75, ch. 5; U.S. Food and Drug Administration,

"Guidance: Potassium Iodide as a Thyroid Blocking Agent in Radiation Emergencies" (Washington, D.C.), www.fda.gov/cder/guidance/index.htm.

9. Lewis A. Dunn, Peter R. Lavoy, and Scott D. Sagan, "Conclusions: Planning the Unthinkable," in *Planning the Unthinkable*, eds. Peter R. Lavoy, Scott D. Sagan, and James J. Wirtz (Ithaca: Cornell University Press, 2000), 239.

10. Abel J. Gonzalez, "Security of Radioactive Sources: The Evolving New International Dimensions," *International Atomic Energy Association Bulletin* 434 (April 2001); Henry Kelly, "Dirty Bombs: Response to a Threat," *Federation of American Scientists Public Interest Report* 55.2 (March/April 2002); Council on Foreign Relations, "Terrorism: Questions and Answers" (New York: 2003), www.terrorismanswers.com, 4 April 2003.

11. Henry Kelly, "Dirty Bombs"; Council on Foreign Relations, "Terrorism: Questions and Answers."

12. Council on Foreign Relations, "Terrorism: Questions and Answers."

13. U.S. Army Field Manual 8-284, "Treatment of Biological Warfare Agent Casualties" (Washington, D.C.: U.S. Army, Navy, and Air Force, and Commandant, Marine Corps, 17 July 2000), sec. 1-1; U.S. Army Field Manual 100-16, "Army Operational Support" (Washington, D.C.: 31 May 1995), ch. 14.

14. U.S. Army Field Manual 8-284, secs 2-1 and 3-1, ch. 4.

15. World Health Organization, *Public Health Response to Chemical and Biological Weapons: WHO Guidance*, 2d ed. (Geneva: November 2001); Council on Foreign Relations, "Terrorism: Questions and Answers."

16. U.S. Army Field Manual 21-75, ch. 5; U.S. Army Field Manual No. 8-284, sec. 1-2.

17. World Health Organization, *Public Health Response*, sec. 3.6.2.

18. U.S. Army Field Manual 8-284, sec. 1-6; William M. Arkin, "A Hazy Target," *Los Angeles Times*, 9 March 2003.

19. World Health Organization, *Public Health Response*; Theodore J. Cieslak and Edward M. Eitzen, Jr., "Bioterrorism: Agents of Concern" in *Public Health Issues in Disaster*, ed. Lloyd F. Novick, (Gaithersburg, Md.: Aspen Publishers, 2001), 79–81; U.S. Army Field Manual 8-284, secs. 2.1–2.10.

20. Theodore J. Cieslak and Edward M. Eitzen, Jr., "Bioterrorism," 80.

21. World Health Organization, *Public Health Response*; Theodore J. Cieslak and Edward M. Eitzen, Jr., "Bioterrorism," 80–1.

22. U.S. Army Field Manual 8-284, sec. 3-6.

23. Theodore J. Cieslak and Edward M. Eitzen, Jr., "Bioterrorism," 82–3.

24. U.S. Army Field Manual 8-284, secs. 3-2–3-3.

25. U.S. Army Field Manual 8-284, secs. 3-6–3-10; World Health Organization, *Public Health Response*, annex 1, 1.4.2; Centers for Disease Control, "Smallpox," www.bt.cdc.gov/agent/smallpox, 4 April 2003; Council on Foreign Relations, "Terrorism: Questions and Answers."

26. Council on Foreign Relations, "Terrorism: Questions and Answers."

27. U.S. Army Field Manual 8-284, secs. 4-2–4-8.

28. U.S. Army Field Manual 8-284, secs. 4-3, 4-6.

29. Robert Gould and Nancy D. Connell, "The Public Health Effects of Biological Weapons," in *War and Public Health*, 100–5; J. Cookson and J. Nottingham,

A Survey of Chemical and Biological Warfare (New York: Monthly Review Press, 1969).

30. U.S. Army Field Manual 8-284, sec. 1-3.

31. U.S. Army Field Manual 21-75, ch. 5.

32. World Health Organization. *Public Health Response*, annex 3, 3.2.

33. U.S. Senate, hearing before the Committee on Foreign Relations, "Reducing the Threat of Chemical and Biological Weapons," 107th Cong., 2d sess., 19 March 2002; World Health Organization, *Health Aspects of Biological and Chemical Weapons*, 2d ed., (Geneva: 17 August 2001), table 3.2.

34. U.S. Army Field Manual 3-100, 1-6–1-7.

35. U.S. Army Field Manual 21-75, ch. 5; U.S. Army Field Manual 3-11.21, "Multiservice Tactics, Techniques, and Procedures for NBC Aspects of Consequence Management" (Washington, D.C.: 12 December 2001), sec. 1-2.6; U.S. Army Field Manual 21-11, "First Aid for Soldiers" (Washington, D.C.: 27 October 1988), sec. 7-6.

36. Alan H. Lockwood, "The Public Health Effects of the Use of Chemical Weapons" in *War and Public Health*, 86–7; U.S. Army Field Manual 21-11, sec. 7-6; Central Intelligence Agency, "The Biological and Chemical Warfare Threat," rev. ed. (Washington, D.C.: 1999).

37. Alan H. Lockwood, "The Public Health Effects," 87–8; Central Intelligence Agency, "The Biological and Chemical Warfare Threat," 29; U.S. Army Field Manual 3-7.

38. Central Intelligence Agency, "The Biological and Chemical Warfare Threat"; U.S. Army Field Manual 3-7, table 2-4.

39. U.S. Army Field Manual 3-7, chs. 2–3.

40. Central Intelligence Agency, "The Biological and Chemical Warfare Threat," 28.

41. Central Intelligence Agency, "The Biological and Chemical Warfare Threat," 29; Kathleen T. Rhem, "We've Got the Nerve" (Alexandria, Va.: Armed Forces Information Service, 1 August 2000).

42. U.S. Army Field Manual 21-11, sec. 7-12.

43. Central Intelligence Agency, "The Biological and Chemical Warfare Threat," 31–2; U.S. Army Field Manual 3-7, ch. 3.

44. World Health Organization, *Health Aspects*, sec. 3.6.2.

45. U.S. Army Field Manual 21-75, sec. 5-6.

46. U.S. Army Field Manual 3-100, sec. 1-6; Anthony G. Macintyre et al., "Weapons of Mass Destruction Events with Contaminated Casualties," *Journal of the American Medical Association*, 283.2 (12 January 2000), U.S. Army Field Manual 3-11.21, sec. 1.2.

47. U.S. Chemical and Biological Defense Program, "Annual Report to Congress and Performance Plan" (Washington, D.C.: U.S. Department of Defense, July 2001); Lewis A. Dunn, Peter R. Lavoy, and Scott D. Sagan, "Conclusions," 231.

48. U.S. Army Field Manual 21-75, sec. 5-7.

49. Franklin D. Jones, "Neuropsychiatric Casualties," 94.

50. U.S. Army Field Manual 22-51, "Leaders' Manual for Combat Stress Control" (Washington, D.C.: 29 September 1994), sec. 1-6.

51. U.S. Army Field Manual 21-75; World Health Organization, *Health Aspects*, executive summary.

52. U.S. Chemical and Biological Defense Program, "Annual Report," intro. III; The Sunshine Project, www.sunshine-project.org, 16 April 2003.

CHAPTER SIX

1. U.S. Army Field Manual 6-22.5, "Combat Stress" (Washington, D.C.: 23 June 2000), secs. 1–4; Dave Grossman, *On Killing: The Psychological Cost of Learning to Kill in War and Society* (Boston: Little, Brown, 1996).

2. U.S. Army Field Manual 22-51, "Leaders' Manual for Combat Stress Control" (Washington, D.C.: 29 September 1994), sec. 2-8.

3. U.S. Army Field Manual 22-51, sec. 2-8.

4. D. Keith Shurtleff, "The Effects of Technology on Our Humanity," *Parameters*, Summer 2002, 100–12.

5. D. Keith Shurtleff, "The Effects of Technology," 100–12.

6. Peter Kilner, "Military Leaders' Obligation to Justify Killing in War," *Military Review*, March–April 2002, 24–31; Erica Goode, "Treatment and Training Help Reduce Stress of War," *New York Times*, 25 March 2003, F1.

7. Harold Kennedy, "Computer Games Liven Up Military Recruiting, Training," *National Defense Magazine*, November 2002; William Hamilton, "Toymakers Study Troops, and Vice Versa," *New York Times*, 30 March 2003, I1.

8. U.S. Army Field Manual 20-3, "Camouflage, Concealment, and Decoys" (Washington, D.C.: 30 August 1999); U.S. Army Field Manual 21-75, "Combat Skills of the Soldier" (Washington, D.C.: 3 August 1984), ch. 1; U.S. Army STP 21-1-SMCT, "Soldier's Manual of Common Tasks, Skill Level 1" (Washington, D.C.: 1 October 1990).

9. U.S. Army Field Manual 3-7, "NBC Field Handbook" (Washington, D.C.: 29 September 1994).

10. U.S. Army Field Manual 22-51, sec. 2-8.

11. Joanna Bourke, *An Intimate History of Killing: Face-to-Face Killing in Twentieth-Century Warfare* (New York: Basic Books, 1999); Dave Grossman, *On Killing*, 231–40.

12. U.S. Army Field Manual 22-51, 2–7; Faris R. Kirkland, Ronald R. Halverson, and Paul D. Bliese, "Stress and Psychological Readiness in Post-Cold War Operations," *Parameters*, Summer 1996, 79–91; J. Glenn Gray, *The Warriors: Reflections on Men in Battle* (New York: Harcourt, Brace, 1959), 161; Dave Grossman, *On Killing*, 75, 243–5.

13. U.S. Army Field Manual 22-51.

14. Dave Grossman and Bruce K. Siddle, "Psychological Effects of Combat," in *Encyclopedia of Violence, Peace, and Conflict*, eds. Lester Kurtz and Jennifer Turpin (San Diego: Academic Press, 1999).

15. David S. Pierson, "Natural Killers: Turning the Tide of Battle," *Military Review*, May 1999; J. Glenn Gray, *The Warriors*, 52; Jack Thompson, "Hidden Enemies," *Soldier of Fortune*, October 1985, 21; R.B. Anderson, "Parting Shot:

Notes

Vietnam Was Fun (?)," *Soldier of Fortune*, November 1988, 96; Dave Grossman, *On Killing*, 231–240.

16. U.S. Army Field Manual 22-51, ch. 3.

17. Joanna Bourke, *An Intimate History of Killing.*

18. U.S. Army Field Manual 22-51, sec. 4-6; Joanna Bourke, *An Intimate History of Killing.*

19. Evan Thomas, "Fear at the Front," *Newsweek*, 3 February 2003, 34.

20. Dave Grossman and Bruce K. Siddle, "Psychological Effects of Combat."

21. Dave Grossman and Bruce K. Siddle, "Psychological Effects of Combat."

22. Dave Grossman, "On Killing II: The Psychological Cost of Learning to Kill," *International Journal of Emergency Mental Health* 3.3 (Summer 2001), 137–44.

23. U.S. Army Field Manual 6-22.5, sec. 2-11.

24. U.S. Army Field Manual 22-51, sec. 3-10.

25. U.S. Army Field Manual 22-51, ch. 2; U.S. Army Field Manual 21-75.

26. U.S. Army Field Manual 6-22.5, sec. 2-5; Evan Thomas, "Fear at the Front"; Ben Shalit, *The Psychology of Conflict and Combat* (New York: Praeger, 1988); J. Glenn Gray, *The Warriors*, 91

27. Elliott V. Converse III et al., "The Exclusion of Black Soldiers from the Medal of Honor in World War II" (Jefferson, N.C.: McFarland and Company, 1997).

28. Harry G. Summers, *Persian Gulf War Almanac* (New York: Facts on File, 1995).

29. James Webb, "Military Competence," speech at Commonwealth Club of California (San Francisco: 28 August 1986), www.jameswebb.com; U.S. Army Center of Military History, "Medal of Honor Citations" (Washington, D.C.: 2002), www.army.mil/cmh-pg/moh1.htm, 9 April 2003.

30. Elliott V. Converse III et al., "The Exclusion of Black Soldiers."

31. Steven J. Eden, "Leadership on Future Fields: Remembering the Human Factor in War," *Military Review*, May–June 1999, 35–8; U.S. Army Field Manual 22-51.

32. U.S. Army Center of Military History, "Medal of Honor Citations."

33. U.S. Army Field Manual 22-51, table A-1; Faris R. Kirkland, Ronald R. Halverson, and Paul D. Bliese, "Stress and Psychological Readiness," 79–91.

34. U.S. Army Field Manual 22-51, sec. 3-10; U.S. Army Field Manual 21-75.

35. U.S. Army Field Manual 21-75, ch. 7.

36. Michael J. Davidson, *A Guide to Military Criminal Law* (Annapolis, Md.: Naval Institute Press, 1999), 142–43; Joint Publication 4-02.2, sec. 1-1.

37. Roger W. Little, "Buddy Relations and Combat Performance," in *The New Military: Changing Patterns of Organization*, ed. Morris Janowitz (New York: Russell Sage Foundation, 1964), 195–223; Joint Publication 4-02.2, "Joint Tactics, Techniques and Procedures for Patient Movement in Joint Operations" (Washington, D.C.: Joint Chiefs of Staff, 30 December 1996), sec. 1-1.

38. David H. Marlowe, *Psychological and Psychosocial Consequences of Combat and Deployment with Special Emphasis on the Gulf War* (MR-1018/11-OSD, Santa Monica, Calif.: RAND, 22 January 2001), table 10.7; Zahava Solomon,

Combat Stress Reaction: The Enduring Toll of War (New York: Plenum Press, 1993), 85–6.

39. U.S. Army Field Manual 6-22.5, sec. 1-4.

40. Center for Army Lessons Learned Handbook 02-8, "Operation Enduring Freedom: Tactics, Techniques, and Procedures" (Ft. Leavenworth, Kans: 2002), sec. 3.

41. Ralph Peters, "Our Soldiers, Their Cities," *Parameters* (Spring 1996), 43–50; U.S. Army Field Manual 20-3, "Camouflage, Concealment, and Decoys" (Washington, D.C.: 30 August 1999); U.S. Army Field Manual 21-75, app. D.

42. U.S. Marine Corps Warfighting Publication 3-35.3, VIII, A-67; Center for Army Lessons Learned Handbook 02-8, ch. 2.

43. Michael J. Davidson, *A Guide to Military Criminal Law*, 144.

44. U.S. Marine Corps Warfighting Publication 3-35.3, "Military Operations on Urban Terrain" (Quantico, Va.: April 1998).

45. U.S. Army Field Manual 90-3, "Desert Operations" (Washington, D.C.: 1993), sec. 3-1.

46. U.S. Army Field Manual 90-5, "Jungle Operations" (Washington, D.C.: 1982), secs. 1-3, 5-1.

47. George Mordica II, "High-Altitude Operations" (Ft. Leavenworth, Kans.: Center for Army Lessons Learned, 2002).

48. U.S. Army Field Manual 6-22.5, sec. 4-1.

49. Center for Army Lessons Learned Handbook 96-3, "Own the Night! Small Unit Night Fighter Manual" (Ft. Leavenworth, Kans.: 1997), ch. 3.

50. Ralph Peters, "The New Warrior Class," *Parameters*, Summer 1994, 16–26.

51. Monte Reel, "Fake Iraqi Surrenders Prompt Changes," *Washington Post*, 26 March 2003, A22; Michael J. Davidson, *A Guide to Military Criminal Law*, 146–47.

52. Michael J. Davidson, *A Guide to Military Criminal Law*, 143.

53. U.S. Army Field Manual 21-75, ch. 6.

54. Michael J. Davidson, *A Guide to Military Criminal Law*, 141–42.

55. Michael J. Davidson, *A Guide to Military Criminal Law*, 68.

56. Dave Grossman, *On Killing*.

57. Uniform Code of Military Justice, Manual for Courts-Martial, app. 2.

58. Cincinnatus (Cecil B. Currey), *Self-Destruction: The Disintegration and Decay of the United States Army During the Vietnam Era* (New York: W.W. Norton, 1981), 155; Richard A. Gabriel and Paul L. Savage, *Crisis in Command: Mismanagement in the Army* (New York: Hill and Wang, 1978), 16.

59. U.S. House, Committee on Appropriations, Subcommittee on Department of Defense, *DOD Appropriations for 1972*, Hearings, 92nd Congress, 1st sess., part 9, May 17–September 23 1971, 585; Richard A. Gabriel and Paul L. Savage, *Crisis in Command: Mismanagement in the Army* (New York: Hill & Wang, 1978), 66–67; Terry H. Anderson, *The Movement and the Sixties* (Oxford: Oxford University Press, 1995), 374; Department of Defense, *Computer Study of Casualties in Vietnam*.

60. U.S. Army Field Manual 22-51, 4–14; Michael J. Davidson, *A Guide to Military Criminal Law*, 135.

61. Philip Caputo, *A Rumor of War* (New York: Henry Holt, 1977); Kenneth K. Steinweg, "Dealing Realistically with Fratricide," *Parameters* 25 (Spring 1995), 4–29.

62. U.S. Army Field Manual 6-22.5, sec. 4-4; U.S. Army Field Manual 21-75.

63. Richard A. Kulka et al., *Trauma and the Vietnam War Generation: Report of Findings from the National Vietnam Veterans Readjustment Study* (New York: Brunner/Mazel, 1990); Karni Ginzburg et al., "Battlefield Functioning and Chronic PTSD: Associations with Perceived Self Efficacy and Causal Attribution," *Personality and Individual Differences* 34.3 (February 2003), 463–76.

64. U.S. Army Field Manual 6-22.5, tables 1-1 and 1-2.

65. U.S. Army Field Manual 6-22.5, sec. 4-4.

66. U.S. Army Field Manual 6-22.5, sec. 2-7.

67. U.S. Army, 528th Medical Detachment, "Combat Stress Frequently Asked Questions" (Fort Bragg, NC: 2003), www.bragg.army.mil/528CSC, 9 April 2003.

68. Faris R. Kirkland, Ronald R. Halverson, and Paul D. Bliese, "Stress and Psychological Readiness," 79–91; U.S. Army Field Manual 22-51, sec. 8-3.

69. U.S. Army Field Manual 22-51, ch. 4.

70. U.S. Army Field Manual 6-22.5, sec. 1.

71. U.S. Army Field Manual 6-22.5, sec. 2-5.

72. Naval Strike and Air Warfare Center NAVMED P-6410, "Performance Maintenance During Continuous Flight Operations: A Guide for Flight Surgeons" (Fallon, Nev.: 1 January 2000).

73. Evan Thomas, "Fear at the Front."

74. Dave Grossman, *On Killing*.

75. U.S. Army Field Manual 6-22.5, sec. 1-3; Dave Grossman and Bruce K. Siddle, "Psychological Effects of Combat"; Evan Thomas, "Fear at the Front."

76. U.S. Army Field Manual 6-22.5, table 1-2.

77. Dave Grossman and Bruce K. Siddle, "Psychological Effects of Combat"; U.S. Army Field Manual 6-22.5, secs. 1–4.

78. Dave Grossman and Bruce K. Siddle, "Psychological Effects of Combat."

79. R.L. Swank and W.E. Marchand, "Combat Neuroses: Development of Combat Exhaustion," *Archives of Neurology and Psychology* 55 (1946), 236–47; Dave Grossman and Bruce K. Siddle, "Psychological Effects of Combat."

CHAPTER SEVEN

1. Edna J. Hunter, "The Psychological Effects of Being a Prisoner of War," in *Human Adaptation to Extreme Stress: From the Holocaust to Vietnam*, eds. John P. Wilson, Zev Harel, and Boaz Kahana (New York: Plenum Press, 1988), 162–3.

2. Edna J. Hunter, "Psychological Effects," 163.

3. U.S. Army Field Manual 21-75, "Combat Skills of the Soldier" (Washington, D.C.: 3 August 1984), app. F.

4. Brian Engdahl and John A. Fairbank, "Former Prisoners of War: Highlights of Empirical Research," in *The Mental Health Consequences of Torture*, eds. Ellen Gerrity et al. (New York: Kluwer Academic/Plenum Publishers, 2001); Edna J. Hunter, "Psychological Effects," 161.

5. Preston John Hubbard, *Apocalypse Undone: My Survival of Japanese Imprisonment During World War II* (Nashville: Vanderbilt University Press, 1990); Edna J. Hunter, "Psychological Effects," 167–8; James B. Stockdale, "Experiences as a POW in Vietnam," *Naval War College Review*, Naval War College Press, Winter 1998.

6. U.S. Department of Defense, Office of the Under Secretary of Defense (Comptroller), "Department of Defense Financial Management Regulation 7000.14R" (Washington, D.C.: 2003), 7A.34–7.

7. Executive Order 10631, "Code of Conduct for Members of the Armed Forces of the United States" (17 August 1955); Edna J. Hunter, "Psychological Effects," 160.

8. Edna J. Hunter, "Psychological Effects," 163–4.

9. Edna J. Hunter, "Psychological Effects," 160; James B. Stockdale, "Experiences as a POW"; Preston John Hubbard, *Apocalypse Undone.*

10. Geneva Conventions of 12 August 1949, Schedule (III) relative to the Treatment of Prisoners of War, art. 48.

11. U.S. Department of Defense, Defense Prisoner of War/Missing Personnel Office, "Personnel Missing—Southeast Asia" (Washington, D.C.: 2003), www.dtic.mil/dpmo/pmsea, 9 April 2003; Thom Shanker and John M. Broder, "The Rescue of Private Lynch: Iraqi's Tip Was a Bugle Call," *New York Times*, 3 April 2003, A10.

12. U.S. Department of Defense Instruction 1300.21, "Code of Conduct (CoC) Training and Education" (Washington, D.C.: 8 January 2001), E2.2.5.1.5.1.

13. U.S. Department of Defense Instruction 1300.21, E2.2.5.2.2.3.

14. Amnesty International, *Torture Worldwide: An Affront to Human Dignity* (New York: Amnesty International Publications, 2000), 32–5.

15. Nigel S. Rodley, *The Treatment of Prisoners Under International Law*, 2d ed. (Oxford: Clarendon Press, 1999), 10.

16. Nigel S. Rodley, *The Treatment of Prisoners*, 10.

17. Nigel S. Rodley, *The Treatment of Prisoners*, 10; Duncan Forrest, "The Methods of Torture and Its Effects," in *A Glimpse of Hell*, ed. Duncan Forrest (New York: New York University Press, 1996), 112.

18. Nigel S. Rodley, *The Treatment of Prisoners*, 7, 8.

19. Amnesty International, *Torture Worldwide*, 33–4.

20. Nigel S. Rodley, *The Treatment of Prisoners*, 9; Edna J. Hunter, "Psychological Effects," 162; Elaine Sciolino, "Female P.O.W. Is Abused, Kindling Debate," *New York Times*, 29 June 1992, A1; Christopher Dickey and Donatella Lorch, "Saddam's Crimes," *Newsweek*, 17 February 2003.

21. Linda Bird Francke, *Ground Zero* (New York: Simon & Schuster, 1997), 91–100.

22. Nigel S. Rodley, *The Treatment of Prisoners*, 10–11.

23. Kate Millett, *The Politics of Cruelty* (New York: W.W. Norton, 1994), 18–9.

24. Kate Millett, *The Politics of Cruelty*, 33–4; Edna J. Hunter, "Psychological Effects," 160.

25. U.S. Army Regulation 190-8, "Enemy Prisoners of War, Retained Personnel, Civilian Internees and Other Detainees" (Washington, D.C.: 1 October 1997);

Dana Priest and Barton Gellman, "U.S. Decries Abuse but Defends Interrogations," *Washington Post*, 26 December 2002, A1; Eric Schmitt, "Ideas and Trends: There Are Ways to Make Them Talk," *New York Times*, 16 June 2002, D1.

26. Nigel S. Rodley, *The Treatment of Prisoners*, 11; James B. Stockdale, "Experiences as a POW."

27. Human Rights Watch, "The Legal Prohibition Against Torture" (New York: 11 March 2003).

28. F.E. Somnier and I.K. Genefke, "Psychotherapy for Victims of Torture," *British Journal of Psychiatry*, 149 (September 1986), 325–7.

29. Sharon Frederick, *Rape: Weapon of Terror* (River Edge, N.J.: Global Publishing Co., 2001); Ruth Seifert, "Rape: The Female Body as a Symbol and a Sign," in *War or Health? A Reader*, eds. Ilkka Taipale et al. (New York: Zed Books, 2002), 280 04.

30. Anne Tierney Goldstein and Margaret A. Schuler, eds., *Gender Violence: The Hidden War Crime* (Washington, D.C.: Women, Law & Development International, 1998), 12; United Nations High Commissioner for Human Rights, U.N. Document E/CN.41995/42, "Preliminary Report Submitted by the Special Rapporteur on Violence Against Women, its Causes and Consequences" (Geneva: November 1994); Mary Elizabeth Ashford and Yolanda Huet-Vaughn, "The Impact of War on Women," in *War and Public Health*, eds. Barry S. Levy and Victor W. Sidel (Washington, D.C.: American Public Health Association, 2000), 189–90; Sharon Frederick, *Rape: Weapon of Terror*.

31. Elisabeth Rehn and Ellen Johnson Sirleaf, "Women, War, and Peace: The Independent Experts' Assessment" (New York: UNIFEM, 2002), 10.

32. Anne Tierney Goldstein and Margaret A. Schuler, eds., *Gender Violence*, 15, 19, 21; Susan Brownmiller, *Against Our Will: Men, Women and Rape* (New York: Ballantine, 1975); Sharon Frederick, *Rape: Weapon of Terror*.

33. Elisabeth Rehn and Ellen Johnson Sirleaf, "Women, War, and Peace," 16; Mary Elizabeth Ashford and Yolanda Huet-Vaughn, "The Impact of War on Women," 190.

34. Madeline Morris, "In War and Peace: Rape, War, and Military Culture," in *War's Dirty Secret: Rape, Prostitution, and Other Crimes Against Women*, ed. Anne Llewellyn Barstow (Cleveland: Pilgrim Press, 2000).

CHAPTER EIGHT

1. Sherwin Nuland, *How We Die* (New York: Vintage Books, 1995), 118–121.

2. Hans Husum, *War Surgery Field Manual* (Penang, Malaysia: Third World Network, 1995), ch. 4.

3. Sherwin Nuland, *How We Die*, 124.

4. Sherwin Nuland, *How We Die*, 16.

5. Sherwin Nuland, *How We Die*, 121.

6. Sherwin Nuland, *How We Die*, 130–1.

7. Robert J. Kastenbaum, *Death, Society, and Human Experience* (New York: Charles E. Merrill Publishing Company, 1986), 140–143

8. Sherwin Nuland, *How We Die*, 122–9.

9. Mark Baker, *Nam: The Vietnam War in the Words of the Men and Women Who Fought There* (New York: Morrow/Avon, 1981), 216.

10. Mark Baker, *Nam*, 242

11. Sherwin Nuland, *How We Die*, 129–33.

12. Sherwin Nuland, *How We Die*, 122–3.

13. Jessica Snyder Sachs, *Corpse: Nature, Forensics, and the Struggle to Pinpoint Time of Death* (Cambridge, Mass.: Perseus Publishing, 2001), 18.

14. Center for Army Lessons Learned, "Killed in Action," *Lessons Learned Newsletter* 1-87 (Ft. Leavenworth, Kans.: 1987).

15. U.S. Army Field Manual 10-286, "Identification of Deceased Personnel" (Washington, D.C.: 1976), sec. 4-8.

16. U.S. Army Field Manual 22-51, "Leaders' Manual for Combat Stress Control" (Washington, D.C.: 29 September 1994), sec. 4-6.

17. International Committee of the Red Cross, "The Missing Members of Armed Forces and Armed Groups: Identification, Family News, Killed in Action and Prevention" (Geneva: 8 August 2002), www.icrc.org, 9 April 2003.

18. U.S. Army Field Manual 22-51, sec. 4-8.

19. Center for Army Lessons Learned, "Killed in Action"; U.S. Army Field Manual 22-51.

20. Total Army Personnel Command, "Casualty Notification Officer Training Program," www-perscom.army.mil, 4 April 2003.

21. U.S. Army Regulation 638–2, "Care and Disposition of Remains and Disposition of Personal Effects" (Washington, D.C.: 2000), C-5–6.

22. U.S. Army Regulation 638-2, C-5–6.

23. William F. Hughes, interview by author, New York, 4 April 2003.

24. U.S. Army Regulation 638-2, ch. 20.

25. U.S. Army Regulation 638-2, ch. 19.

26. U.S. Army Regulation 638-2, ch. 20.

27. U.S. Army Regulation 638-2, secs. 12-1, 12-4(b) 3.

28. U.S. Army Regulation 638-2, C-5–6; Arlington Cemetery, "A Guide to Burial at Arlington National Cemetery" (Arlington, Va.: 2003), www.arlingtoncemetery.org, 4 April 2003.

29. U.S. Department of Veterans Affairs, "2004 Departmental Performance Plan" (Washington, D.C.: 2003), www.va.gov, 4 April 2003.

30. Arlington Cemetery, "A Guide to Burial."

31. U.S. Marine Corps, "What's Next? A Guide to Family Readiness" (Jenkintown, Penn: Educational Publications, Inc., 1998).

32. Arlington Cemetery, "A Guide to Burial."

33. U.S. Department of Veterans Affairs, "Facts About the National Cemetery Administration" (Washington, D.C.: December 2002), www.va.gov, 4 April 2003.

34. Arlington Cemetery, "A Guide to Burial."

35. U.S. Department of Veterans Affairs, "Facts About the National Cemetery Administration"; U.S. Department of Veterans Affairs, "2004 Departmental Performance Plan."

36. U.S. Department of Veterans Affairs, "Facts About the National Cemetery Administration."

37. Robert J. Kastenbaum, *Death, Society, and Human Experience*, 149–51.

38. Robert J. Kastenbaum, *Death, Society, and Human Experience*, 140–3.

39. Barbara A. Backer, Natalie Hannon, and Noreen A. Russell, *Death and Dying: Understanding and Care* (Albany: Delmar Publishers, 1994), 276–7.

CHAPTER NINE

1. David H. Marlowe, *Psychological and Psychosocial Consequences of Combat and Deployment with Special Emphasis on the Gulf War* (MR-1018/11-OSD, Santa Monica, Calif.: RAND, 2000), 124.

2. U.S. Army Field Manual 6-22.5, "Combat Stress" (Washington, D.C.: 23 June 2000), sec. 2-7.

3. David H. Marlowe, *Psychological and Psychosocial Consequences*, 125.

4. U.S. Army Community and Family Support Center, Operation READY, "The Soldier/Family Deployment Survival Handbook" (Washington, D.C.: 2002), 12.

5. Simon H. Pincus et al., "The Emotional Cycle of Deployment: A Military Family Perspective" (Falls Church, Va.: Office of the Army Surgeon General, the U.S. Army Center for Health Promotion and Preventive Medicine, the Army National Guard, and the Office of the Chief, Army Reserve, 2003), www.hooah4health.com, 4 April 2003.

6. Sandra A. Yerkes and Harry C. Holloway, "War and Homecoming: The Stressors of War and of Returning From War," in *Emotional Aftermath of the Persian Gulf War: Veterans, Families, Communities, and Nations*, eds. Robert J. Ursano and Ann E. Norwood (Washington, D.C.: American Psychiatric Press, 1996), 25–42; Wilbur J. Scott, "PTSD and Agent Orange: Implications for a Sociology of Veterans' Issues," *Armed Forces and Society* 18.4 (Summer 1992), 592–612; Committee on Veterans' Affairs, "A Study of the Problems Facing Vietnam Era Veterans on Their Readjustment to Civilian Life" (Washington, D.C.: U.S. Government Printing Office, 1972).

7. Jerry Lembcke, *The Spitting Image: Myth, Memory, and the Legacy of Vietnam* (New York: New York University Press, 1998); Committee on Veterans' Affairs, "A Study of the Problems," 75.

8. Wilson Ring, "Some National Guard Members Receive Abuse from Public," Associated Press, 27 March 2003; Jerry Lembcke, *The Spitting Image*, 6, 71–83; A. D. Horne, ed., *The Wounded Generation: America After Vietnam* (Englewood Cliffs, NJ: Prentice-Hall, 1981), 114–5.

9. Jerry Lembcke, *The Spitting Image*, 115–16.

10. David H. Marlowe, *Psychological and Psychosocial Consequences*, 150.

11. U.S. Army Field Manual 6-22.5, sec. 2-7; U.S. Army Community and Family Support Center, "Survival Handbook," 30.

12. U.S. Army Field Manual 6-22.5, sec. 2-7; Simon H. Pincus et al., "The Emotional Cycle of Deployment."

13. Jose Florante J. Leyson, "Psychosexual Scars of Recent Wars," in *The Military Family in Peace and War*, ed. Florence W. Kaslow (New York: Springer Publishing Company, 1993); Simon H. Pincus et al., "The Emotional Cycle of Deployment"; U.S. Army Community and Family Support Center, "Survival Hand-

book," 30; T. Ishøy et al., "Prevalence of Male Sexual Problems in the Danish Gulf War Study," *Scandinavian Journal of Sexology* 4.1 (March 2001), 43–55.

14. Simon H. Pincus et al., "The Emotional Cycle of Deployment."

15. U.S. Army Community and Family Support Center, "Survival Handbook," 17.

16. Kimberly A. Lee et al., "A 50-Year Prospective Study of the Psychological Sequelae of World War II Combat," *American Journal of Psychiatry* 152.4 (April 1995), 516–22; J.D. Hamilton and R.H. Workman, "Persistence of Combat-Related Posttraumatic Stress Symptoms for 75 Years," *Journal of Traumatic Stress* 11.4 (October 1998), 763–8; Nigel Hunt and Ian Robbins, "The Long-Term Consequences of War: The Experience of World War II," *Aging and Mental Health* 5.2 (May 2001), 184–91.

17. Joseph A. Boscarino, "Diseases Among Men 20 Years After Exposure to Severe Stress: Implications for Clinical Research and Medical Care," *Psychosomatic Medicine* 59.6 (November–December 1997), 605–14.

18. Thomas C. Neylan, "Sleep Disturbances in the Vietnam Generation: Findings from a Nationally Representative Sample of Male Vietnam Veterans," *American Journal of Psychiatry* 155.7 (July 1998), 929–33; D.L. Dlugosz et al., "Risk Factors for Mental Disorder Hospitalization After the Persian Gulf War: U.S. Armed Forces, June 1, 1991–September 30, 1993," *Journal of Clinical Epidemiology* 52.12 (1999), 1267–78.

19. Dave Grossman and Bruce K. Siddle, "Psychological Effects of Combat," in *Encyclopedia of Violence, Peace, and Conflict* (San Diego: Academic Press, 1999), 159.

20. Steven M. Southwick et al., "Trauma-Related Symptoms in Veterans of Operation Desert Storm: A 2-Year Follow-Up," *American Journal of Psychiatry* 152.8 (1995), 1150–5; N. Breslau and G.C. Davis, "Posttraumatic Stress Disorder: The Etiology of Specific Wartime Stressors," *American Journal of Psychiatry* 144 (1987), 578–83.

21. Angela Pereira, "Combat Trauma and the Diagnosis of Post-Traumatic Stress Disorder in Female and Male Veterans," *Military Medicine* 167.1 (January 2002), 23–7; Alan Fontana and Robert A. Rosenheck, "Duty-Related and Sexual Stress in the Etiology of PTSD Among Women Veterans Who Seek Treatment," *Psychiatric Services* 49.5 (1998) 658–62; N. Breslau et al., "Sex Differences in PTSD," *Archives of General Psychiatry* 54.11 (1997), 1044–8.

22. Richard A. Kulka et al., *Trauma and the Vietnam War Generation: Report of Findings from the National Vietnam Veterans Readjustment Study* (New York: Brunner/Mazel, 1990).

23. B.K. Jordan et al., "Problems in Families of Male Veterans with Post-Traumatic Stress Disorder," *Journal of Consulting and Clinical Psychology* 60.6 (1992), 916–26.

24. C.M. Chemtob et al., "Head Injury and Combat-Related Stress Disorder," *The Journal of Nervous and Mental Disease* 186.11 (November 1998), 701–8.

25. Jennifer J. Vasterling, Kevin Brailey, and Patricia B. Sutker, "Olfactory Identification in Combat-Related Posttraumatic Stress Disorder," *Journal of Traumatic Stress* 13.2 (April 2000), 241–54; K.T. Mueser and R.W. Butler, "Audi-

tory Hallucinations in Combat-Related Chronic Posttraumatic Stress Disorder," *American Journal of Psychiatry* 144 (1987), 299–302.

26. Arturo J. Silva et al., "Dangerous Misidentification of People Due to Flashback Phenomena in Posttraumatic Stress Disorder," *Journal of Forensic Sciences* 43.6 (November 1998), 1107–11.

27. Steven M. Southwick et al., "Consistency of Memory for Combat-Related Traumatic Events in Veterans of Operation Desert Storm," *American Journal of Psychiatry* 154.2 (February 1997), 173–7.

28. Matthew J. Friedman, "Posttraumatic Stress Disorder: An Overview" (Washington, D.C.: National Center for PTSD, U.S. Department of Veterans Affairs), www.ncptsd.org/facts/general/fs_overview.html, 7 April 2003.

29. Wilbur J. Scott, "PTSD and Agent Orange," 592–612; Kenneth C. Hyams, F. Stephen Wignall, and Rovert Roswell, "War Syndromes and Their Evaluation: From the U.S. Civil War to the Persian Gulf War," *Annals of Internal Medicine* 125 (1996), 398–405; Eric T. Dean, *Shook Over Hell: Post-Traumatic Stress, Vietnam, and the Civil War* (Cambridge, Mass.: Harvard University Press, 1997), 16–17; Saul Bloom et al., eds., *Hidden Casualties: Environmental, Health, and Political Consequences of the Persian Gulf War* (Berkeley, Calif.: North Atlantic Books, 1994).

30. Eric T. Dean, *Shook Over Hell*, 18.

31. U.S. Department of Veterans Affairs, "Overview of Homelessness" (Washington, D.C.: 15 November 2002), www.va.gov, 4 April 2003.

32. U.S. Department of Veterans Affairs, "Federal Benefits for Veterans and Dependents (2003 Edition)" (Washington, D.C.: 2003), www.va.gov, 4 April 2003.

33. The Congressional Medal of Honor Society (Mt. Pleasant, S.C.: 2003).

34. National World War II Memorial, www.wwiimemorial.com, 5 April 2003.

35. Diana M. Elliott, "Traumatic Events: Prevalence and Delayed Recall in the General Population," *Journal of Consulting and Clinical Psychology* 65.5 (October 1997), 811–20.

36. Alan Fontana et al., "Psychological Benefits and Liabilities of Traumatic Exposure in the War Zone," *Journal of Traumatic Stress* 11.3 (July 1998), 485–503.

37. Roger Little, "Friendships in the Military Community," in *Research in the Interweave of Social Roles: Friendship* Vol. 2 (Greenwich, Conn.: Jai Press, 1981), 221–35; J. Glenn Gray, *The Warriors: Reflections On Men in Battle* (New York: Harcourt, Brace, 1959), 89–90.

38. Scott Air Force Base, "Retiree Archive or Library," sub-section 2.19, public.scott.af.mil/375aw/rao, 5 April 2003; U.S. Army Regulation 670-1, "Wear and Appearance of Army Uniforms and Insignia" (Washington, D.C.: 1 July 2002), 322 6.

39. Scott Air Force Base, "Retiree Archive or Library," sub-section 2.19; Army Regulation 670-1, 322–6.

BIBLIOGRAPHY

Alvarez, Alex. *Governments, Citizens, and Genocide: A Comparative and Interdisciplinary Approach.* Bloomington: Indiana University Press, 2001.

Amnesty International. *Torture Worldwide: An Affront to Human Dignity.* New York: Amnesty International Publications, 2000.

Anderson, R.B. "Parting Shot: Vietnam Was Fun (?)," *Soldier of Fortune,* November 1988, 96.

Arlington Cemetery. "A Guide to Burial at Arlington National Cemetery." Arlington, Va.: www.arlingtoncemetery.org, 4 April 2003.

Asch, Beth, James R. Hosek, Jeremy Arkes, C. Christine Fair, Jennifer Sharp, and Mark Totten, *Military Recruiting and Retention After the Fiscal Year 2000 Pay Legislation.* MR-1532-OSD, Santa Monica, Calif.: RAND, 2002.

Arkin, William M. "A Hazy Target." *Los Angeles Times,* 9 March 2003.

Backer, Barbara A., Natalie Hannon, and Noreen A. Russell. *Death and Dying: Understanding and Care.* Albany: Delmar Publishers Inc., 1994.

Baker, Jason B. "A Jump to Celebrate," *Soldiers* 57:6 (June 2002), 27.

Baker, Mark. *Nam : The Vietnam War in the Words of the Men and Women Who Fought There.* New York: Morrow/Avon, 1981.

Bartlett, Craig S. "Clinical Update: Gunshot Wound Ballistics." *Clinical Orthopaedics and Related Research* 408 (2003), 28–57. Baskir, Lawrence M. and William A. Strauss. *Chance and Circumstance.* New York: Alfred A. Knopf, 1978.

Bastian, Lisa D., Anita R. Lancaster, and Heidi E. Reyst. "Department of Defense 1995 Sexual Harassment Survey." Arlington, Va.: Defense Manpower Data Center, December 1996.

Bauman, Christian. Interview by author, New York, 4 April 2003.

Bellamy, Ronald F. and Russ Zajtchuk, eds. *Conventional Warfare: Ballistic, Blast, and Burn Injuries.* Falls Church, Va.: Office of the Army Surgeon General, 1989.

Belmont, Jr., Philip J., et al. "Incidence, Epidemiology, and Occupational Outcomes of Thoracolumbar Fractures Among U.S. Army Aviators." *Journal of Trauma Injury, Infection, and Critical Care* 50.5 (2001), 855–61.

Bloom, Saul, et al., eds. *Hidden Casualties: Environmental, Health, and Political Consequences of the Persian Gulf War.* Berkeley, Calif.: North Atlantic Books, 1994.

Boscarino, Joseph A. "Diseases Among Men 20 Years After Exposure to Severe Stress: Implications for Clinical Research and Medical Care." *Psychosomatic Medicine* 59.6 (November–December 1997), 605–14.

Bourke, Joanna. *An Intimate History of Killing: Face-to-Face Killing in Twentieth-Century Warfare.* New York: Basic Books, 1999.

Bousfield, Chrissie Bosworth, ed. *Burn Trauma: Management and Nursing Care.* Philadelphia: Whurr Publishers, 2002.

Bray, Robert M. "1998 Department of Defense Survey of Health Related Behaviors Among Military Personnel." Research Triangle Park, N.C.: Research Triangle Institute, 1999.

Bray, Robert M. "1998 Department of Defense Survey of Health Related Behaviors Among Military Personnel." Research Triangle Park, N.C.: Research Triangle Institute, 1999.

Breslau, N., et al. "Sex Differences in PTSD." *Archives of General Psychiatry* 54.11 (1997), 1044–48.

Breslau, N. and G.C. Davis. "Posttraumatic Stress Disorder: The Etiology of Specific Wartime Stressors." *American Journal of Psychiatry* 144 (1987), 578–83.

Brownmiller, Susan. *Against Our Will: Men, Women and Rape.* New York: Ballantine, 1975.

Bryant, Clifton D. *Khaki Collar Crime: Deviant Behavior in the Military Context.* New York: Free Press, 1979.

Buddin, Richard J., Carole Roan Gresenz, Susan D. Hosek, Marc N. Elliott, and Jennifer Hawes-Dawson. *An Evaluation of Housing Options for Military Families.* MR-1020-OSD, Santa Monica, Calif.: RAND, 1999.

Campbell, Kenneth J. *Genocide and the Global Village.* New York: Palgrave, 2001.

Caputo, Philip. *A Rumor of War.* New York: Henry Holt and Company, 1977.

Carey, Michael. "Analysis of Wounds Incurred by U.S. Army Seventh Corps Personnel Treated in Corps Hospitals During Operation Desert Storm, February 20 to March 10, 1991." *Journal of Trauma: Injury, Infection, and Critical Care* 40.3 (1996), Supplement 165–68.

Carey, Michael et al. "Ballistic Helmets and Aspects of Their Design." *Neurosurgery* 47 (2000), 678–89.

Carlton, Eric. *Massacres: An Historical Perspective.* Brookfield, Vt.: Ashgate Publishing Company, 1994.

Center for Army Lessons Learned. "Killed in Action." *Lessons Learned Newsletter.* Ft. Leavenworth, Kans.: (1-87) 1987.

———. Handbook 02-8. "Operation Enduring Freedom: Tactics, Techniques, and Procedures." Ft. Leavenworth, Kans.: 2002.

———. Handbook 96-3. "Own the Night! Small Unit Night Fighter Manual." Ft. Leavenworth, Kans.: 1997.

Center for Responsive Politics. "Defense: Long-Term Contribution Trends." Washington, D.C.: 2003.

Center for Strategic and Budgetary Assessments. "Federal Spending and the Gross Domestic Product." Washington, D.C.: February 2002.

Centers for Disease Control. "Smallpox." Atlanta, www.bt.cdc.gov/agent/smallpox, 4 April 2003.

Central Intelligence Agency. "The Biological and Chemical Warfare Threat," rev. ed. Washington, D.C.: 1999.

Cernak, Ibolja et al. "Blast Injury From Explosive Munitions." *Journal of Trauma: Injury, Infection, and Critical Care* 47.1 (1999), 96–103.

Chemtob, C.M., et al. "Head Injury and Combat-Related Stress Disorder." *The Journal of Nervous and Mental Disease* 186.11 (November 1998), 701–8.

Cieslak, Theodore J., and Edward M. Eitzen, Jr. "Bioterrorism: Agents of Concern." In *Public Health Issues in Disaster.* Ed. Lloyd F. Novick. Gaithersburg, Md.: Aspen Publishers, 2001.

Cincinnatus (Cecil B. Currey). *Self-Destruction: The Disintegration and Decay of the United States Army During the Vietnam Era.* New York: W.W. Norton, 1981.

Committee on Veterans Affairs. "A Study of the Problems Facing Vietnam Era Veterans on Their Readjustment to Civilian Life." Washington, D.C.: U.S. Government Printing Office, 1972.

Committee to Review the Health Consequences of Service During the Persian Gulf War. *Health Consequences of Service During the Persian Gulf War: Recommendations for Research and Information Systems.* Washington, D.C.: National Academy Press, 1996.

Congressional Medal of Honor Society. "Medal of Honor Recipients." Mt. Pleasant, S.C.: www.cmohs.org, 16 April 2003.

Converse, III, Elliott V., et al. "The Exclusion of Black Soldiers from the Medal of Honor in World War II." Jefferson, N.C.: McFarland and Company, 1997.

Council on Foreign Relations. "Terrorism: Questions and Answers." New York: www.terrorismanswers.com, 4 April 2003.

Covey, Dana C., et al. "Field Hospital Treatment of Blast Wounds of the Musculoskeletal System During the Yugoslav Civil War." *Journal of Orthopaedic Trauma* 14.4 (2000), 278–86.

Dashkina, Antonina. "The System of Social Support and Help to Ex-Officers and Their Families in Great Britain, the United States of America and Russia." Brussels: NATO Academic Forum Fellowship, 1996.

Davidson, Michael J. *A Guide to Military Criminal Law.* Annapolis, Md.: Naval Institute Press, 1999.

Dean, Eric T. *Shook Over Hell: Post-Traumatic Stress, Vietnam, and the Civil War.* Cambridge, Mass.: Harvard University Press, 1997.

Defense Manpower Data Center. "2002 Active Duty Status of Forces Survey: Overview Briefing." Arlington, Va.: 31 January 2003.

Defense Technical Information Center. "Basic Allowance for Housing." Fort Belvoir, Va.: 2000.

Dickey, Christopher, and Donatella Lorch. "Saddam's Crimes," *Newsweek,* 17 February 2003.

Disaster Preparedness Handbook. Loudon, NH: Turning Point Communications. www.disastermagazine.com, 11 April 2003.

Di Maio, Vincent J.M. In *Gunshot Wounds: Practical Aspects of Firearms, Ballistics, and Forensic Techniques*. New York: Elsevier, 1985.

Dlugosz, D.L., et al. "Risk Factors for Mental Disorder Hospitalization After the Persian Gulf War: U.S. Armed Forces, June 1, 1991–September 30, 1993." *Journal of Clinical Epidemiology* 52.12 (1999), 1267–78.

Dunn, Lewis A., Peter R. Lavoy, and Scott D. Sagan. "Conclusions: Planning the Unthinkable." In *Planning the Unthinkable*. Eds. Peter R. Lavoy, Scott D. Sagan, and James J. Wirtz. Ithaca: Cornell University Press, 2000.

Durante, Marco, and Mariagabriella Pugliese. "Estimates of Radiological Risk from Depleted Uranium Weapons in War Scenarios." *Health Physics* 82.1 (January 2002), 14–20.

Eden, Steven J. "Leadership on Future Fields: Remembering the Human Factor in War." *Military Review*, May–June 1999.

Elliott, Diana M. "Traumatic Events: Prevalence and Delayed Recall in the General Population." *Journal of Consulting and Clinical Psychology* 65.5 (October 1997), 811–20.

Ender, Morten G., ed. *Military Brats and Other Global Nomads: Growing Up in Organization Families*. Westport, Conn.: Praeger, 2002.

Engdahl, Brian, and John A. Fairbank. "Former Prisoners of War: Highlights of Empirical Research." In *The Mental Health Consequences of Torture*. Ed. Ellen Gerrity et al. New York: Kluwer Academic/Plenum Publishers, 2001.

Etcheson, Craig. *The Rise and Demise of Democratic Kampuchea*. Boulder: Westview Press, 1984.

Executive Order 10631. "Code of Conduct for Members of the Armed Forces of the United States." 17 August 1955.

Federation of American Scientists. "Special Weapons Primer." www.fas.org/nuke/intro.

———, Arm Sales Monitoring Project. "2002 Notifications to Congress of Pending U.S. Arms Transfers." Washington, D.C.: 2002.

Fitzpatrick, James E. "Superficial Fungal Skin Diseases." In *Military Dermatology, Part III: Disease and the Environment*. Eds. William D. James and Russ Zajtchuck. Washington, D.C.: Office of the Army Surgeon General, 1994.

Fontana, Alan, et al. "Psychological Benefits and Liabilities of Traumatic Exposure in the War Zone." *Journal of Traumatic Stress* 11.3 (July 1998), 485–503.

Fontana, Alan, and Robert A. Rosenheck. "Duty-Related and Sexual Stress in the Etiology of PTSD Among Women Veterans Who Seek Treatment." *Psychiatric Services* 49.5 (1998), 658–62.

Forrest, Duncan. "The Methods of Torture and Its Effects." In *A Glimpse of Hell*. Ed. Duncan Forrest. New York: New York University Press, 1996.

Frederick, Sharon, *Rape: Weapon of Terror*. River Edge, N.J.: Global Publishing Co., 2001.

Friedman, Matthew J. "Posttraumatic Stress Disorder: An Overview." Washington, D.C.: National Center for PTSD, U.S. Department of Veterans Affairs. www.ncptsd.org/facts/general/fs_overview.html, 7 April 2003.

Bibliography

Gabriel, Richard A., and Paul L. Savage. *Crisis in Command: Mismanagement in the Army.* New York: Hill and Wang, 1978.

Garcia, Victoria. "A Risky Business: U.S. Arms Exports to Countries Where Terror Thrives." Washington, D.C.: Center for Defense Information, 29 November 2001.

Geier, Joel. "Vietnam: The Soldier's Rebellion." *International Socialist Review,* 9 (Fall 1999), 38–48.

Geneva Conventions of 12 August 1949, Schedule (III) relative to the Treatment of Prisoners of War.

Gilmore, Gerry J. "Recruit Attrition Rates Fall Across the Services." Alexandria, Va.: Armed Forces Information Service, 13 August 2001.

Ginzburg, Karni, et al. "Battlefield Functioning and Chronic PTSD: Associations with Perceived Self Efficacy and Causal Attribution." *Personality and Individual Differences* 34.3 (February 2003), 463–76.

Glantz, David M. *The Battle for Leningrad, 1941–1944.* Lawrence: University of Kansas Press, 2002.

Gofrit, O.N., et al. "Accurate Anatomical Location of War Injuries: Analysis of the Lebanon War Fatal Casualties and the Proposition of New Principles for the Design of Military Personal Armour System." *Injury* 27.8 (October 1996), 577–8.

Goldstein, Anne Tierney, and Margaret A. Schuler, eds. *Gender Violence: The Hidden War Crime.* Washington, D.C.: Women, Law & Development International, 1998.

Goldstein, Joshua S. *War and Gender: How Gender Shapes the War System and Vice Versa.* Cambridge: Cambridge University Press, 2001.

Goode, Erica. "Treatment and Training Help Reduce Stress of War." *New York Times,* 25 March 2003, F1.

Gonzalez, Abel J. "Security of Radioactive Sources: The Evolving New International Dimensions." *International Atomic Energy Association Bulletin* 434 (April 2001), 39–48.

Gottlieb, Sherry Gershon. *Hell No, We Won't Go! Resisting the Draft During the Vietnam War.* New York: Penguin, 1991.

Gray, J. Glenn. *The Warriors: Reflections on Men in Battle.* New York: Harcourt, Brace, 1959.

Grimmett, Richard F. "Conventional Arms Transfer to Developing Nations, 1994–2001." Washington, D.C.: Congressional Research Service. fpc.state.gov/documents/organization/12632.pdf, 6 August 2002.

Grossman, Dave. *On Killing: The Psychological Cost of Learning to Kill in War and Society.* Boston: Little, Brown, 1995.

———. "On Killing II: The Psychological Cost of Learning to Kill." *International Journal of Emergency Mental Health* 3.3 (Summer 2001), 137–44.

Grossman, Dave, and Bruce K. Siddle. "Psychological Effects of Combat." In *Encyclopedia of Violence, Peace, and Conflict.* Eds. Lester Kurtz and Jennifer Turpin. San Diego: Academic Press, 1999.

Gunby, P. "Service in Strict Islamic Nation Removes Alcohol, Other Drugs from Major Problem List." *Journal of the American Medical Association* 265 (1991), 560.

Halbfinger, David M., and Steven A. Holmes. "Military Mirrors a Working-Class America." *New York Times*, 30 March 2003, A1.

Hamilton, J.D., and R.H. Workman. "Persistence of Combat-Related Posttraumatic Stress Symptoms for 75 Years." *Journal of Traumatic Stress* 11.4 (October 1998), 763–68.

Hamilton, William. "Toymakers Study Troops, and Vice Versa." *New York Times*, 30 March 2003, I1.

Harrell, Margaret, et al. *Barriers to Minority Participation in Special Operations Forces.* MR-1042-SOCOM, Santa Monica, Calif.: RAND, 1999.

Harrell, Margaret C., and Laura L. Miller. *New Opportunities for Military Women: Effects Upon Readiness, Cohesion, and Morale.* MR-896-OSD, Santa Monica, Calif.: RAND, 1997.

Hartung, William D., and Frida Berrigan. "U.S. Arms Transfers and Security Assistance to Israel." New York: Arms Trade Resource Center, World Policy Institute, 6 May 2002.

Higate, Paul Richard. "Theorizing Continuity: From Military to Civilian Life." *Armed Forces and Society* 27.3 (Spring 2001), 443–60.

Hinton, Alexander Laban, ed. *Annihilating Difference: The Anthropology of Genocide.* Berkeley: University of California Press, 2002.

Horne, A.D., ed. *The Wounded Generation: America After Vietnam.* Englewood Cliffs, N.J.: Prentice-Hall, 1981.

Hosek, James, Beth Asch, C. Christine Fair, Craig Martin, and Michael Mattock. *Married to the Military: The Employment and Earnings of Military Wives Compared with Those of Civilian Wives.* MR-1565-OSD, Santa Monica, Calif.: RAND, 2002.

Hosek, Susan D., et al. *Minority and Gender Differences in Officer Career Progression.* MR-1184-OSD, Santa Monica, Calif.: RAND, 2001.

Hubbard, Preston John. *Apocalypse Undone: My Survival of Japanese Imprisonment During World War II.* Nashville: Vanderbilt University Press, 1990.

Huber, Thomas M. "Deception: Deceiving the Enemy in Operation Desert Storm." In *Combined Arms Battle Since 1939.* Ed. Roger J. Spiller. Ft. Leavenworth, Kans.: U.S. Army Command and General Staff College Press, 1992. Hughey, Michael John. "The Health Care of Women in Military Settings." *Operational Obstetrics & Gynecology*, 2d ed. NAVMEDPUB 6300-2D, 1 January 2000. www.vnh.org, 4 April 2003.

Hughes, William F. Interview by author, New York, 4 April 2003.

Human Rights Watch. "The Anfal Campaign Against the Kurds: A Middle East Watch Report." New York: 1993.

———. "The Legal Prohibition Against Torture." New York: 11 March 2003.

Hunt, Nigel, and Ian Robbins. "The Long-Term Consequences of War: The Experience of World War II." *Aging and Mental Health* 5.2 (May 2001), 183–90.

Hunter, Edna J. "The Psychological Effects of Being a Prisoner of War." In *Human Adaptation to Extreme Stress: From the Holocaust to Vietnam.* Eds. John P. Wilson, Zev Harel, and Boaz Kahana. New York: Plenum Press, 1988.

Bibliography

Husum, Hans. *War Surgery Field Manual*. Penang, Malaysia: Third World Network, 1995.

Hyams, Kenneth C., et al. "The Impact of Infectious Diseases on the Health of U.S. Troops Deployed to the Persian Gulf During Operations Desert Shield/ Desert Storm." *Clinical Infectious Diseases* 20 (1995), 1497–504.

Hyams, Kenneth C., F. Stephen Wignall, and Rovert Roswell. "War Syndromes and Their Evaluation: From the U.S. Civil War to the Persian Gulf War." *Annals of Internal Medicine* 125 (1996), 398–405.

Ibarguen, Diego. "Bush Sees 2 Marines Wounded in Iraq Become U.S. Citizens," *Philadelphia Inquirer*, 11 April 2003

International Committee of the Red Cross. "The Missing/Members of Armed Forces and Armed Groups: Identification, Family News, Killed in Action and Prevention." Geneva. www.icrc.org, 9 April 2003.

Ishøy, T., et al. "Prevalence of Male Sexual Problems in the Danish Gulf War Study." *Scandinavian Journal of Sexology* 4.1 (March 2001), 43–55.

Joint Chiefs of Staff. "Joint Tactics, Techniques and Procedures for Patient Movement in Joint Operations," Joint Publication 4-02.2, Washington, D.C.., 30 December 1996.

Joint Service Committee on Military Justice. "Manual for Courts-Martial, United States, 2000 Edition." Washington, D.C.: 2000.

Jones, B.H.A., and B.C. Hansen, eds. *Injuries in the Military: A Hidden Epidemic*. Aberdeen Proving Ground, MD: U.S. Army Center for Health Promotion and Preventive Medicine, 1996.

Jones, Franklin D. "Neuropsychiatric Casualties of Nuclear, Biological, and Chemical Warfare." In *Textbook of Military Medicine*. Eds. Franklin D. Jones et al. Washington, D.C.: Office of the Army Surgeon General, 1995.

Jordan, B.K., et al. "Problems in Families of Male Veterans with Post-Traumatic Stress Disorder." *Journal of Consulting and Clinical Psychology* 60.6 (1992), 916–26.

Kaslow, Florence W., ed. *The Military Family in Peace and War*. New York: Springer Publishing Company, 1993.

Kastenbaum, Robert J. *Death, Society, and Human Experience*. New York: Charles F. Merrill Publishing Company, 1986.

Keeler, Jill R. "Pyridostigmine Used as a Nerve Agent Pretreatment Under Wartime Conditions." *Journal of the American Medical Association* 286.5 (7 August 1991), 694–5.

Kellett, Anthony. *Combat Motivation: The Behavior of Soldiers in Battle*. Boston: Kluwer, 1982.

Kelly, Henry. "Dirty Bombs: Response to a Threat." *Federation of American Scientists Public Interest Report* 55.2 (March/April 2002).

Kennedy, Harold. "Computer Games Liven Up Military Recruiting, Training." *National Defense Magazine*, November 2002.

Khan, M. Tahir, et al. "Hindfoot Injuries Due to Landmine Blast Accidents." *Injury* 33 (2002), 167–71.

Kilner, Peter. "Military Leaders' Obligation to Justify Killing in War." *Military Review* (March–April 2002).

Kimenyi, Alexandre and Otis L. Scott, eds. *Anatomy of Genocide: State-Sponsored Mass-Killings in the Twentieth Century.* Lewiston, N.Y.: Edwin Mellen Press, 2001.

Kirkland, Faris R., Ronald R. Halverson, and Paul D. Bliese. "Stress and Psychological Readiness in Post–Cold War Operations." *Parameters* 26:2 (Summer 1996), 79–91.

Kulka, Richard A., et al. *Trauma and the Vietnam War Generation: Report of Findings from the National Vietnam Veterans Readjustment Study.* New York: Brunner/Mazel, 1990.

Larson, Eric V. "Casualties and Consensus: The Historical Role of Casualties in Domestic Support for U.S. Military Operations." MR-726-OSD, Santa Monica, Calif.: RAND, 1996.

Layton, Lyndsey. "Navy Women Finding Ways to Adapt to a Man's World." *Washington Post,* 15 March 2003, A15.

Lee, Kimberly A., et al. "A 50-Year Prospective Study of the Psychological Sequelae of World War II Combat." *American Journal of Psychiatry* 152.4 (April 1995), 516–22.

Lembcke, Jerry. *The Spitting Image: Myth, Memory, and the Legacy of Vietnam.* New York: New York University Press, 1998.

Levy, Barry S., and Victor W. Sidel, eds. *War and Public Health.* Washington, D.C.: American Public Health Association, 2000.

Little, Roger W. "Buddy Relations and Combat Performance." In *The New Military.* Ed. Morris Janowitz. New York: Russell Sage Foundation, 1964.

———. "Friendships in the Military Community." In *Research in the Interweave of Social Roles: Friendship* vol. 2. Greenwich, Conn.: JAI Press, 1981, 221–35.

Lyons, James. "Heat in Gulf to Rocket." London *Daily Mirror,* 2 April 2003.

Mabry, Robert L., et al. "United States Army Rangers in Somalia: An Analysis of Combat Casualties on an Urban Battlefield." *The Journal of Trauma: Injury, Infection, and Critical Care* 49.3 (2000), 515–29.

Machel, Graca. *The Impact of War on Children.* London: Hurst & Company, 2001.

Macintyre, Anthony G., et al. "Weapons of Mass Destruction Events with Contaminated Casualties." *Journal of the American Medical Association* 283.2 (12 January 2000).

Malkasian, Carter. *The Korean War: 1950–1953.* Chicago, Ill.: Fitzroy Dearborn, 2001.

Mangum, Stephen L., and David E. Ball. "Military Skill Training: Some Evidence of Transferability." *Armed Forces and Society* 13.3 (Spring 1987), 425–41.

Marlowe, David H. *Psychological and Psychosocial Consequences of Combat and Deployment with Special Emphasis on the Gulf War.* MR-1018/11-OSD, Santa Monica, Calif.: RAND, 22 January 2001.

Marriott, Bernadette M., ed. *Food Components to Enhance Performance, Committee on Military Nutrition Research.* Washington, D.C.: Food and Nutrition Board, 1994.

McCormick, David. *The Downsized Warrior: America's Army in Transition.* New York: New York University Press, 1998.

Melman, Seymour. *After Capitalism: From Managerialism to Workplace Democracy.* New York: Alfred A. Knopf, 2001.

Military Family Resource Center. "2001 Demographics: Profile of the Military Community." Arlington, Va.: 2002.

Millett, Kate. *The Politics of Cruelty.* New York: W.W. Norton, 1994.

Monga, Manoj, et al. "Gunshot Wounds to the Male Genitalia." *The Journal of Trauma: Injury, Infection, and Critical Care* 38.6 (1995), 855–58.

Mordica, George II. "High-Altitude Operations." Ft. Leavenworth, Kans.: Center for Army Lessons Learned, 2002.

Morris, Madeline. "In War and Peace: Rape, War, and Military Culture." In *War's Dirty Secret: Rape, Prostitution, and Other Crimes Against Women.* Ed. Anne Llewellyn Barstow. Cleveland: Pilgrim Press, 2000.

Moskos, Charles C. "Army Women." *Atlantic Monthly* 266.2 (August 1990), 71–8.

———. *The American Enlisted Man: The Rank and File in Today's Military.* New York: Russell Sage Foundation, 1970.

Moskos, Charles C., and John Sibley Butler. *All That We Can Be: Black Leadership and Racial Integration the Army Way.* New York: Basic Books, 1996.

Mueser, K.T., and R.W. Butler. "Auditory Hallucinations in Combat-Related Chronic Posttraumatic Stress Disorder." *American Journal of Psychiatry* 144 (1987), 299–302.

National Center for Health Statistics. "Births, Marriages, Divorces, and Deaths: Provisional Data for January–December 2000." *National Vital Statistics Reports* 49.6 (22 August 2001).

National Defense Research Institute, *Sexual Orientation and U.S. Military Personnel Policy: Options and Assessment.* MR-323-OSD, Santa Monica, Calif.: RAND, 1993.

National World War II Memorial. www.wwiimemorial.com, 5 April 2003.

Naval Strike and Air Warfare Center. "Performance Maintenance During Continuous Flight Operations: A Guide for Flight Surgeons." NAVMED P-6410, Fallon, Nevada. 1 January 2000.

Neylan, Thomas C. "Sleep Disturbances in the Vietnam Generation: Findings from a Nationally Representative Sample of Male Vietnam Veterans." *American Journal of Psychiatry* 155.7 (July 1998), 929–33.

Nofi, Al. "Statistical Summary: America's Major Wars." www.cwc.lsu.edu/cwc/other/stats/warcost.htm, 4 April 2003.

Nordhaus, William. "The Economic Consequences of a War with Iraq." In *War with Iraq: Costs, Consequences, and Alternatives.* Cambridge, Mass.: American Academy of Arts and Sciences, 2002, 57–95.

Nuclear Weapons: Report of the Secretary-General of the United Nations. London: Frances Pinter, 1981.

Nuland, Sherwin. *How We Die.* New York: Vintage Books, 1995.

Orwell, George. "The Spanish Civil War: Wounded by a Fascist Sniper, near Huesca, 20 May 1937." In *Eyewitness to History.* Ed. John Carey. Cambridge, Mass.: Harvard University Press, 1988.

Parker, Jay. Interview, West Point, N.Y., 22 April 2003.

Peker, Ahmet Fuat, et al. "Penile Reconstruction with Prosthesis and Free Skin Graft in a Patient with Land Mine Blast Injury." *The Journal of Urology* 167 (2002), 2133–34.

Pereira, Angela. "Combat Trauma and the Diagnosis of Post-Traumatic Stress Disorder in Female and Male Veterans." *Military Medicine* 167.1 (January 2002), 23–7.

Peters, Ralph. "Our Soldiers, Their Cities." *Parameters* 26:1 (Spring 1996), 43–50.
———. "The New Warrior Class." *Parameters* 24:2 (Summer 1994), 16–26.

Pierson, David S. "Natural Killers: Turning the Tide of Battle." *Military Review* (May 1999), 60–65.

Pincus, Simon H., et al. "The Emotional Cycle of Deployment: A Military Family Perspective." *U.S. Army Medical Department Journal* April–June 2001.

Popovich, Rose M., John W. Gardner, Robert Potter, Joseph J. Knapik, and Bruce H. Jones. "Effect of Rest from Running on Overuse Injuries in Army Basic Training." *American Journal of Preventive Medicine* 18.3, Supplement 1 (April 2000), 147–55.

Priest, Dana. "Pregnancy Often Causes Tension in Army's Ranks." *Washington Post*, 30 December 1997, A6.

Priest, Dana, and Barton Gellman. "U.S. Decries Abuse but Defends Interrogations." *Washington Post*, 26 December 2002, A1.

Quester, Aline O., and Curtis L. Gilroy. "America's Military: A Coat of Many Colors." Alexandria, Va.: Center for Naval Analysis, July 2001.

Radine, Lawrence B. *The Taming of the Troops: Social Control in the United States Army.* Westport, Conn.: Greenwood Press, 1977.

Rehn, Elisabeth, and Ellen Johnson Sirleaf. "Women, War, and Peace: The Independent Experts' Assessment." New York: UNIFEM, 2002.

Reel, Monte. "Fake Iraqi Surrenders Prompt Changes." *Washington Post*, 26 March 2003, A22.

Rhem, Kathleen T. "We've Got the Nerve." Alexandria, Va.: Armed Forces Information Service, 1 August 2000.

Ring, Wilson. "Some National Guard Members Receive Abuse from Public." Associated Press, 27 March 2003.

Rodley, Nigel S. *The Treatment of Prisoners Under International Law*, 2d ed. Oxford: Clarendon Press, 1999.

Rokke, Douglas, former head of the Pentagon's Depleted Uranium Project, untitled remarks. Washington, D.C.: The National Vietnam and Gulf War Veterans Coalition 17th Annual Leadership Breakfast, U.S. Senate Caucus Room, 10 November 2000.

Ruger, William, Sven E. Wilson, and Shawn L. Waddoups. "Warfare and Welfare: Military Service, Combat, and Marital Dissolution." *Armed Forces & Society* 29.1 (Fall 2002), 85–107.

Sachs, Jessica Snyder. *Corpse: Nature, Forensics, and the Struggle to Pinpoint Time of Death.* Cambridge, Mass.: Perseus Publishing, 2001.

Sarron, Jean-Claude et al. "Consequences of Nonpenetrating Projectile Impact on a Protected Head: Study of Rear Effects of Protections." *The Journal of Trauma: Injury, Infection, and Critical Care* 49.5 (November 2000), 923–29.

Bibliography

Schmidt, Susan, and Vernon Loeb. "'She Was Fighting to the Death': Details Emerging of W. Va. Soldier's Capture and Rescue." *Washington Post*, 3 April 2003, A01.

Schmitt, Eric. "Ideas and Trends: There Are Ways to Make Them Talk." *New York Times*, 16 June 2002, D1.

Sciolino, Elaine. "Female POW Is Abused, Kindling Debate." *New York Times*, 29 June 1992, A1.

Scott Air Force Base. "Retiree Archive or Library." public.scott.af.mil/375aw/rao, 5 April 2003.

Scott, Wilbur J. "PTSD and Agent Orange: Implications for a Sociology of Veterans' Issues." *Armed Forces and Society* 18.4 (Summer 1992), 592–612.

Servicemembers Legal Defense Network. "Conduct Unbecoming: The Ninth Annual Report on 'Don't Ask, Don't Tell, Don't Pursue, Don't Harass.'" Washington, D.C.: 2003.

Shalit, Ben. *The Psychology of Conflict and Combat.* New York: Praeger, 1988.

Shanker, Thom, and John M. Broder. "The Rescue of Private Lynch: Iraqi's Tip Was a Bugle Call." *New York Times*, 3 April 2003, A10.

Shaw, R. Paul, and Yuwa Wang. *Genetic Seeds of Warfare: Evolution, Nationalism, and Patriotism.* Boston: Unwin Hyman, 1989.

Shilts, Randy. *Conduct Unbecoming: Lesbians and Gays in the U.S. Military.* New York: St. Martin's Press, 1993.

Shurtleff, D. Keith. "The Effects of Technology on Our Humanity." *Parameters* 32:2 (Summer 2002), 100–122.

Silva, Arturo J., et al. "Dangerous Misidentification of People Due to Flashback Phenomena in Posttraumatic Stress Disorder." *Journal of Forensic Sciences* 43.6 (November 1998), 1107–11.

Simons, Anna. *The Company They Keep: Life Inside the U.S. Army Special Forces.* New York: Free Press, 1997.

Sivard, Ruth Leger. *World Military and Social Expenditures 1991.* Washington, D.C.: World Priorities, 1991.

Smith, Daniel. "The World at War—January 2003." *Defense Monitor* 32:1 (January–February 2003).

Solomon, Zahava. *Combat Stress Reaction: The Enduring Toll of War* (New York: Plenum Press, 1993), 85–6.

Somnier, F.E., and I.K. Genefke. "Psychotherapy for Victims of Torture." *British Journal of Psychiatry*, 149 (September 1986), 325–27.

Southwick, Steven M., et al. "Consistency of Memory for Combat-Related Traumatic Events in Veterans of Operation Desert Storm." *American Journal of Psychiatry* 154.2 (February 1997), 173–77.

Southwick, Steven M., et al. "Trauma-Related Symptoms in Veterans of Operation Desert Storm: A 2-Year Follow-Up." *American Journal of Psychiatry* 152.8 (1995), 1150–55.

Spiers, Edward M. *Weapons of Mass Destruction.* New York: St. Martin's Press, 2000.

Steinweg, Kenneth K. "Dealing Realistically with Fratricide." *Parameters* 25:1 (Spring 1995), 4–29.

Stiner, Carl, Tony Koltz, and Tom Clancy. *Shadow Warriors: Inside the Special Forces*. New York: Putnam, 2002.

Stockdale, James B. "Experiences as a POW in Vietnam." *Naval War College Review* (Winter 1998).

Summers, Harry G. *Persian Gulf War Almanac*. New York: Facts on File, 1995.

Sunshine Project, The. www.sunshine-project.org, 16 April 2003.

Swank, R.L., and W.E. Marchand. "Combat Neuroses: Development of Combat Exhaustion." *Archives of Neurology and Psychology* 55 (1946), 236–47.

Taipale, Ilkka, ed. *War or Health? A Reader*. New York: Zed Books, 2002.

Ternus, Mona P. "Bosnia and Kosovo: Aeromedical Evacuation in the Initial Stages of Deployment." *Aviation, Space, and Environmental Medicine*, 72.4 (April 2001), 357–60..

Thayer, Thomas C. *War Without Fronts: The American Experience in Vietnam*. Boulder, Colo.: Westview Press, 1985.

Thomas, Evan. "Fear at the Front." *Newsweek*, 3 February 2003, 34.

Thompson, Jack. "Hidden Enemies," *Soldier of Fortune*, October 1985, 21.

Toner, James H. *Morals Under the Gun: The Cardinal Virtues, Military Ethics, and American Society*. Lexington: University Press of Kentucky, 2000.

Total Army Personnel Command. "Casualty Notification Officer Training Program." www.perscom.army.mil, 4 April 2003.

United Nations General Assembly. "Convention Against Torture and Other Cruel, Inhuman or Degrading Treatment or Punishment." General Assembly resolution 39/46, Article XV, New York, 4 February 1985.

———. "Convention on the Prevention and Punishment of the Crime of Genocide." Resolution 260 (III) A, 9 December 1948, Paris, article II.

United Nations High Commissioner for Human Rights. "Preliminary Report Submitted by the Special Rapporteur on Violence Against Women, its Causes and Consequences." U.N. Document E/CN.41995/42, Geneva, 1994.

United Nations High Commissioner for Refugees. "Refugees Flee in All Directions as Conflict Spreads in Eastern Liberia." www.unhcr.ch, 3 April 2003.

———. "The State of the World's Refugees 2000: 50 Years of Humanitarian Action." Oxford: Oxford University Press, 2002.

U.S. Air Force Instruction 36-3003. "Military Leave Program." Washington, D.C.: 14 April 2000.

U.S. Army, 528th Medical Detachment. "Combat Stress Frequently Asked Questions." Fort Bragg, NC: 2003. www.bragg.army.mil/528CSC, 9 April 2003.

U.S. Army, Army Fact File. "M-4 Carbine." Washington, D.C.: www.army.mil/fact_files_site, 9 April 2003.

U.S. Army Center for Health Promotion and Preventative Medicine. "Depleted Uranium—Human Exposure and Health Risk Characterization in Support of the Environmental Exposure Report 'Depleted Uranium in the Gulf' of the Office of the Special Assistant to the Secretary of Defense for Gulf War Illnesses, Medical Readiness, and Military Deployment." Falls Church, Va., September 2000. www.gulflink.osd.mil, 7 April 2003.

U.S. Army Center of Military History. "Medal of Honor Citations." Washington, D.C.: 2002. www.army.mil/cmh-pg/moh1.htm, 9 April 2003.

Bibliography

U.S. Army Community and Family Support Center, Operation READY. "The Soldier/Family Deployment Survival Handbook." Washington, D.C: 2002.

U.S. Army Corps of Engineers. "Fact Sheet: Use ordnance safety precautions at the Camp Robinson Formerly Used Defense Site," Little Rock: September 2001, 1–2.

U.S. Army Correspondence Program CM2307. "Nuclear Reporting." Washington, D.C.: 1 June 1997. U.S. Army Family Liason Office. "Frequently Asked Questions." www.aflo.org, 4 April 2003.

———. "Chemical and Biological Operations." CM7114, Washington, D.C.: 1 January 1995.

U.S. Army Family Liason Office. "Frequently Asked Questions." www.aflo.org, 4 April 2003.

U.S. Army Headquarters. "Care and Disposition of Remains and Disposition of Personal Effects." Regulation 638-2, Washington, D.C.: 2000.

———. "Enemy Prisoners of War, Retained Personnel, Civilian Internees and Other Detainees." Regulation 190-8, Washington, D.C.: 1 October 1997.

———. Field Manual 3-7, "NBC Field Handbook." Washington, D.C.: 29 September 1994.

———. Field Manual 3-11.21, "Multiservice Tactics, Techniques, and Procedures for NBC Aspects of Consequence Management." Washington, D.C.: 12 December 2001.

———. Field Manual 3-100, "Chemical Operations Principles and Fundamentals." Washington, D.C.: 8 May 1996.

———. Field Manual 6-22.5, "Combat Stress." Washington, D.C.: 23 June 2000.

———. Field Manual 8-284, "Treatment of Biological Warfare Agent Casualties." Washington, D.C.: 17 July 2000.

———. Field Manual 10-286, "Identification of Deceased Personnel." Washington, D.C.: 1976.

———. Field Manual 20-3, "Camouflage, Concealment, and Decoys." Washington, D.C.: 30 August 1999.

———. Field Manual 21-11, "First Aid for Soldiers." Washington, D.C.: 27 October 1988.

———, Field Manual 21-20, "Physical Fitness Training." Washington, D.C.: 30 September 1992.

———. Field Manual 21-75, "Combat Skills of the Soldier." Washington, D.C.: 3 August 1984.

———. Field Manual 22-51, "Leaders' Manual for Combat Stress Control." Washington, D.C.: 29 December 1994.

———. Field Manual 90-3, "Desert Operations." Washington, D.C.: 1993.

———. Field Manual 90-5, "Jungle Operations." Washington, D.C.: 1982.

———. Field Manual 100-16, "Army Operational Support." Washington, D.C.: 31 May 1995.

———. "Soldier's Manual of Common Tasks, Skill Level 1." Washington, D.C.: 1 October 1990.

———. "Standards of Medical Fitness." Regulation 40-501, Washington, D.C.: 30 September 2002.

————. "Wear and Appearance of Army Uniforms and Insignia." Regulation 670-1, Washington, D.C.: 1 July 2002.

U.S. Army John F. Kennedy Special Warfare Center and School. "Special Forces Pipeline." Key West, Fla.: www.soc.mil/swcs/museum/Pipeline.shtml, 9 April 2003.

U.S. Army Recruiting Command. "FY 2002 Demo Profile." Ft. Knox, Ky.: 2002.

U.S. Army TRADOC, "Army Training." Regulation 350-1, Ft. Monroe, Va.: 1 August 1983.

————. "Enlisted Initial Entry Training (IET) Policies and Administration." Regulation 350-6, Ft. Monroe, Va.: 3 July 2001.

U.S. Bureau of the Census. *Census 2000.* Washington, D.C.

U.S. Central Command. "Prohibited Activities for U.S. Department of Defense Personnel Serving in the United States Central Command." www.centcom.mil, 4 April 2003.

U.S. Defense Finance and Accounting Service. "Basic Pay—Effective January 1, 2003." Washington, D.C.

————. "Complete Active Duty and Reserve Monthly Drill Pay Tables, 2001." Washington, D.C.

U.S. Department of Defense. "Active Duty Military Personnel by Rank/Grade." Washington, D.C.: 31 January 2003, web1.whs.osd.mil/mmid/military/ms11.pdf, 16 April 2003.

————. "Code of Conduct (CoC) Training and Education." Instruction 1300.21, Washington, D.C.: 8 January 2001.

————. "Defense Almanac." Washington, D.C.: 2003. www.defenselink.mil/pubs/almanac, 16 April 2003

————. Defense Prisoner of War/Missing Personnel Office. "Personnel Missing—Southeast Asia." Washington, D.C.: www.dtic.mil/dpmo/pmsea, 9 April 2003.

————. "Defense Science Board Task Force on Quality of Life." Washington, D.C.: 1995.

————. "Department of Defense Postal Manual." 4525.6-M, Washington, D.C.: 15 August 2002.

————. Deployment Health Support Directorate, Depleted Uranium Information Library. Falls Church, Va., 2002. deploymentlink.osd.mil/du_library, 4 April 2003.

————. "DoD Top 100 Companies and Their Subsidiaries, Fiscal Year 2002." Washington, D.C.

————. "Employment of Spouses of Active Duty Military Members Stationed Worldwide." Instruction 1404.12, Washington, D.C.: 12 January 1989.

————. "Information Paper: Vaccine Use During the Gulf War." Washington, D.C.: 7 December 2000. www.gulflink.osd.mil/va, 4 April 2003.

————. "Leave and Liberty." Directive 1327.5, Washington, D.C.: 10 September 1997.

————. "Military Casualty Information." Washington, D.C.: 15 March 2003. http://web1.whs.osd.mil/mmid/casualty/castop.htm, 16 April 2003.

————. "National Defense Budget Estimates for FY2003." Washington, D.C.: 2002. www.defensedaily.com/budgets/fy03_greenbook.pdf, 9 April 2003.

————. "The Ninth Quadrennial Review of Military Compensation, 2001." Washington, D.C.

————. Office of the Under Secretary of Defense (Comptroller). "Financial Management Regulation 7000.14R" (Washington, D.C.: 2003), 7A.34–7.

————. "Qualification Standards for Enlistment, Appointment, and Induction." Directive 1304.26, Washington, D.C.: 21 December 1993.

U.S. Department of Homeland Security. "Chemical Weapons Fact Sheet." Washington, D.C.: 10 February 2003.

U.S. Department of State. "Military Expenditures and Arms Transfers 1999–2000." Washington, D.C.: March 2003. www.state.gov/documents/organization/18725. pdf, 25 March 2003.

U.S. Department of Veterans Affairs. "America's Wars Fact Sheet." Washington, D.C.: May 2001. www.va.gov/pressrel/amwars01.htm, 16 April 2003

————. "Facts About the National Cemetery Administration." Washington, D.C.: December 2002. www.va.gov, 4 April 2003.

———— "Federal Benefits for Veterans and Dependents, 2003 Edition." Washington, D.C.: 2003. www.va.gov, 4 April 2003.

————, National Center for PTSD. "What Is Posttraumatic Stress Disorder? A National Center for PTSD Fact Sheet." Washington, D.C.: October 2002. http://www.ncptsd.org/faq.html, 2 April 2003.

————. "Overview of Homelessness." Washington, D.C.: 15 November 2002. www.va.gov, 4 April 2003.

————. "2004 Departmental Performance Plan." Washington, D.C.: 2003. www. va.gov, 4 April 2003.

U.S. Food and Drug Administration. "Guidance: Potassium Iodide as a Thyroid Blocking Agent in Radiation Emergencies." Washington, D.C.: November 2001, www.fda.gov/cder/guidance/index.htm, 16 April 2003

U.S. General Accounting Office. "Gender Issues: Information on DOD's Assignment Policy and Direct Ground Combat Definition." GAO-NSIAD-99-7, Washington, D.C.: October 1998.

————. "Military Personnel: Longer Time Between Moves Related to Higher Satisfaction and Retention." Washington, D.C.: August 2001.

U.S. Marine Corps. "What's Next? A Guide to Family Readiness." Jonkintown, Pa.: Educational Publications, Inc., 1998.

————. Equipment Factfile. "M-16A2 5.56mm Rifle." Washington, D.C.: 15 December 1995 www.hqmc.usmc.mil, 16 April 2003.

————. "Military Operations on Urban Terrain." Warfighting Publication 3-35.3, Quantico, Va.: April 1998.

U.S. Navy. "Navy Special Warfare," www.sealchallenge.navy.mil, 14 April 2003

U.S. Office of Management and Budget. "Budget of the United States Government, Fiscal Year 2004." Washington, D.C.: 3 February 2003.

U.S. Office of the Assistant Secretary of Defense (Force Management Policy). "Population Representation in the Military Services, Fiscal Year 1999." Washington, D.C.: November 2000.

U.S. Office of the Under Secretary of Defense for Personnel and Readiness. "Military Compensation." Washington, D.C.: 2003. dod.mil/militarypay, 1 April 2003

Ursano, Robert J. and Ann E. Norwood, eds. *Emotional Aftermath of the Persian Gulf War: Veterans, Families, Communities, and Nations.* Washington, D.C.: American Psychiatric Press, 1996.

Vasterling, Jennifer J., Kevin Brailey, and Patricia B. Sutker. "Olfactory Identification in Combat-Related Posttraumatic Stress Disorder." *Journal of Traumatic Stress* 13.2 (April 2000), 241–54.

Vaughan, Don. "Relying on Luck." *The Retired Officer Magazine,* November 2002.

Vernon, Alex. *The Eyes of Orion: Five Tank Lieutenants in the Persian Gulf War.* Kent, Ohio: Kent State University Press, 1999.

Watson, Peter. *War on the Mind: The Military Uses and Abuses of Psychology.* New York: Basic Books, 1978.

Webb, James. "Military Competence." Speech at Commonwealth Club of California. San Francisco: 28 August 1986. www.jameswebb.com, 16 April 2003.

Wilson, Michael J., James B. Greenlees, Tracey Hagerty, D. Wayne Hintze, and Jerome D. Lehnus. "Youth Attitude Tracking Study 1998: Propensity and Advertising Report,." Rockville, Md.: Westat, Inc. and Arlington, Va.: Defense Manpower Data Center, 17 January 2000.

Williams, Rudi. "Chu Says Benefits Are Good, but Improvements Can Be Made." Alexandria, Va.: Armed Forces Information Service, 24 May 2002.

World Health Organization. "Communicable Diseases: Surveillance and Response." www.who.int, 14 April 2003.

———. *Health Aspects of Biological and Chemical Weapons,* 2d ed. Geneva: 2001.

———. *Public Health Response to Chemical and Biological Weapons: WHO Guidance,* 2d ed. Geneva: 2001.

ACKNOWLEDGMENTS

These people were instrumental in editing and shaping the book:

Christian Bauman enlisted in the U.S. Army in 1991 and left as a specialist (E-4) in 1995, serving four years in the small Waterborne field. He deployed for expeditionary service twice, to Somalia (1992–1993) with a platoon from the 1098th Medium Boat Co., and Haiti (1994) with the LSV-1 detachment. The author of *The Ice Beneath You* (Scribner, 2002), he lives and works in New Hope, Pennsylvania.

Carolyn Hughes Copenhaver graduated from West Point in 1992, and served in military intelligence until 1997, when she left the service as a captain. From 1993 to 1996 she was stationed at Fort Bragg, North Carolina, where she served as counterintelligence platoon leader, company operations officer, battalion assistant operations officer, and headquarters company executive officer in the 519th Military Intelligence Battalion. A senior-rated jumpmaster, she was deployed to Haiti with the 519th in 1994. In 1996 and 1997 she served as Division Collection Manager in the 311th Military Intelligence Battalion at Fort Campbell, Kentucky. Carolyn is currently a research analyst for Presearch, Incorporated, in Charlottesville, Virginia.

Sam Frank has worked for *Harper's*, dustedmagazine.com, and the *Chicago Reader.* He is a native of Hoboken, New Jersey, and a graduate of Yale University.

Cabe Franklin is a freelance writer and researcher. A graduate of Amherst College, he has worked for the White House Office of News Analysis, the U.S. Senate Sergeant at Arms, and *Harper's* magazine. He lives in New York City.

Dr. William F. Hughes graduated from West Point in 1966 and retired from the U.S. Army as a colonel. He served three tours in Vietnam, as a second lieutenant, first lieutenant, and captain, and was decorated with a Silver Star, Distinguished Flying Cross, Purple Heart, Air Medal (37 Awards), and Combat Infantry Badge. He is a lifetime member of the 75th Ranger Regiment and was the founding command surgeon of U.S. Special Operations Command.

John R. Hughes graduated from West Point in 1996, and currently serves as a captain in the U.S. Army Medical Corps. He is a resident in emergency medicine at Fort Hood, Texas. He is a flight surgeon, and Airborne/Ranger qualified. He was deployed in 1997 to Haiti, where he served as an infantry platoon leader with the 504th Parachute Infantry Regiment of the 82nd Airborne Division.

Laurie Kelliher is a freelance journalist based in New York. She has been published in *The New York Times* and New York *Daily News.* She is a graduate of Kenyon College and of the Columbia Graduate School of Journalism.

Byrd Schas is a New York–based journalist currently freelancing for *New York* magazine. She was an editorial assistant at Golden Books, an intern at the Committee to Protect Journalists, and has a B.A. (English) from Barnard College and master's in journalism from New York University.

Jarrad Shiver enlisted in the U.S. Marine Corps after graduating from high school in Yukon, Oklahoma, in 1990. He spent four years on active duty and three years as an active reservist, all with the infantry, and left the service in 1998 as a sergeant

(E-5). He has been awarded the Good Conduct Medal, National Defense Service Medal, and the Sea Service Deployment Ribbon. He is currently studying for a bachelor's degree in history and economics at the University of Texas at Austin.

John P. Wheeler III, West Point 1966, was Captain, General Staff, HQ, U.S. Army Vietnam 1969–70. His section ran the computer network that controlled logistics and manpower in the war zone. In the office of the secretary of defense and on the Joint Staff he was an expert on nuclear, chemical, and biological warfare and contributed directly to the presidential decision that the U.S. will not use biological weapons. He served Presidents Ronald Reagan and George H. W. Bush in several posts and advised the 2000 campaign of President George W. Bush. He chaired the Vietnam Veterans Memorial Fund, which built the Wall; was first chairman and CEO of Mothers Against Drunk Driving; and is president of the Vietnam Children's Fund, a charity that builds schools in Vietnam. His father, John P. Wheeler Jr., West Point January 1943, led in creating the M-1 Abrams tank and the Bradley fighting vehicle.

Paul Woodruff served in Vietnam, as a first lieutenant and later as a captain, in MACV (Military Assistance Command, Vietnam). He served there in IV Corps from June 1969 to June 1970, and later taught at Fort Bragg. After earning his Ph.D. in philosophy in 1973, he joined the philosophy department at the University of Texas at Austin, where he has served ever since. He is currently director of the university's Plan II honors program as well as the faculty liaison for the ROTC programs on campus. His most recent book is *Reverence: Renewing a Forgotten Virtue.*

I am also indebted to assistance from Ben Monnie, Johnny Dwyer, Chris Hawke, Laura Longhine, Noah Reibel and Ashley Chapman, students at the Columbia Graduate School of Journalism. Nir Rosen, Reed Jackson, Christian Lorentzen, and Jennifer MacNeil helped us check facts on short notice.

Dominick Anfuso, Martha Levin, Nancy Inglis, and Wylie O'Sullivan at Free Press were of great assistance. I look forward to working with them on my next book.

Lisa Bankoff of International Creative Management was again instrumental in getting my idea onto the printed page.

The staff at New York University's Bobst Library, where the research for this book was done, helped us daily. I want to thank Carol Sternhell and Cathleen Dullahan at New York University, who facilitated with kindness and speed the permissions for the researchers to use Bobst Library.

INDEX

ABOUT THE AUTHOR

CHRIS HEDGES has been a foreign correspondent for fifteen years. He joined the staff of *The New York Times* in 1990 and previously worked for *The Dallas Morning News*, *The Christian Science Monitor*, and National Public Radio. He holds a B.A. in English literature from Colgate University and a master of divinity from Harvard University. He is Lecturer in the Council of the Humanities and Ferris Professor of Journalism at Princeton University. Hedges was a member of the *New York Times* team that won the 2002 Pulitzer Prize for Explanatory Reporting for the paper's coverage of global terrorism, and he received the 2002 Amnesty International Global Award for Human Rights Journalism. He is the author of *War Is a Force That Gives Us Meaning*, which was a finalist for the National Book Critics Circle Award. He lives in New York City.